J. Stacey

A prince in Israel

Or, sketches of the life of John Ridgway

J. Stacey

A prince in Israel
Or, sketches of the life of John Ridgway

ISBN/EAN: 9783743355200

Manufactured in Europe, USA, Canada, Australia, Japa

Cover: Foto ©Lupo / pixelio.de

Manufactured and distributed by brebook publishing software (www.brebook.com)

J. Stacey

A prince in Israel

SKETCHES

OF THE

LIFE OF JOHN RIDGWAY, ESQ.

Faithfully yours
Jno Ridgway

A PRINCE IN ISRAEL;

OR,

SKETCHES

OF THE

LIFE OF JOHN RIDGWAY, ESQ.

BY THE

REV. J. STACEY,

AUTHOR OF "THE CHRISTIAN SACRAMENTS," "THE CHURCH AND THE AGE," ETC.

LONDON:
HAMILTON, ADAMS, AND CO.,
PATERNOSTER ROW.

MDCCCLXII.

LONDON: BENJAMIN PARDON, PRINTER, PATERNOSTER ROW.

PREFACE.

THIS volume should have appeared some time ago. The delay is but in a slight degree attributable to the author. When requested to prepare it there was little human probability that he would ever be able even to commence the task. He was then only in the first stage of recovery from an illness which had threatened to be fatal, and which still held him prostrate and helpless. Even under favourable circumstances several months must elapse before the first step could be taken, in fulfilment of the request; while a full half year from the death of Mr. Ridgway had expired before the request was made. The favourable circumstances were graciously given. A shattered health was gradually built up again, if not to robustness, yet to a moderate working capability; in recollection of which the author desires thus formally to acknowledge the tender mercy of God, and at the same time never to forget the vows that were spoken by him when he was in trouble. Still, recovery was sufficiently protracted to make much mental application perilous, and labour of almost any kind burdensome: while the strength slowly gained was wanted for duties which claimed, and therefore received, the first attention. Delay was thus inevitable. But this delay has not been without advantage. Though it may have somewhat injured the circulation desired for the work, it has certainly tended in some degree to its greater completeness.

Of the work itself the author may not speak, save to remark, that he has sought, by means of such information as he possessed, to preserve for general instruction the memory of one of those, of whom the number is happily increasing in every Christian denomination, who, raised by successful commercial enterprise to a position of wealth and social influence, employ their advantages, not as luxuries to be appropriated in selfish gratification, but as talents to be used in the common interests of humanity and religion. The life of such a one, if written with any due share of appreciation and fidelity, must have something to say which all may hear with profit, though most to say to those who are in circumstances of worldly prosperity similar to his own. To these then especially the work is commended, though not as furnishing a perfect model for their imitation; for who, whatever his character, can pretend to this height of perfection? but as indicating, in more than one respect, and particularly in those respects which are highest, the line of conduct they would do well to pursue.

"The leaders of industry," says a great living sage, "are the captains of the world." To this class of commanders Mr. Ridgway belonged, and he accepted the command, or at least finally held it, with no narrow and selfish views of its duties and responsibilities. The object of his leading was not primarily to make a fortune, or to found a family. It was not even to develop a particular branch of trade, or to give employment and means of subsistence to numbers of individuals dependent on his enterprise and skill, praiseworthy as unquestionably this latter object would have been. It was rather, by means of accumulating resources and greater public and private influence, to further those higher interests of man and society, to which material advantages should ever be held subservient; to gain, in fact, both power and position, that from some high vantage ground, and in a sense eminently moral and religious, as well as social and political, he might the more effectually serve his generation according to the will of God, and then peacefully fall on sleep. And this object he accomplished, and accomplished it so as to have, if not in any one great exploit, or in a plurality of such, yet in the multitude and manifold variety of his labours—persevered in to the close of a long life—much wherewith to meet the demand with which the great Napoleon is said to have challenged the capacity or desert of any one who was commended to him for employment or reward—" What has he done ?" It is for this reason that the present memoir is written; and for the further reason, related to this, that the commemoration of such a life as Mr. Ridgway lived may tend to form to a similar and even higher excellence many other lives.

The memoir is necessarily, to some extent, denominational. The author, however, persuades himself that it will not in any restrictive, much less in any uncharitable sense, be found sectarian.

To several friends his acknowledgments are due for suggestions, letters, &c.; but to one in particular—Mr. William Scott, of Barlaston—whose friendship he values as one of the peculiar blessings of his life.

BROOM GROVE, SHEFFIELD,
    October, 1862.

CONTENTS.

CHAPTER I.

EMINENT MEN CENTRES OF HISTORIC INTEREST.

The Man and the Occasion—Luther—Wesley—Methodism Rich in Biography—Christianity in Earnest—John Ridgway, a Prince in Israel ....*Page* 3

CHAPTER II.

NATURAL ENDOWMENTS AND HOME INFLUENCES.

Early and Late Deaths—Natural Gifts—Relation of Mind to Body—A Christian Home—True Nobility—The Ridgway Family—Conversion of Father—His Exemplary Character—A Helpmeet—Piety in the Bud—A Painful Portrait—A Merry Childhood—Natural Frankness—Sport, and Something else—The Young Ornithologist—Perils and Escapes—Providential Oversight—Sage Advice—Raw Material of Excellence ....*Page* 15

CHAPTER III.

THE SUCCESSFUL MANUFACTURER.

Schools and Schoolmasters—From School to Business—Work a Divine Ordinance—To Labour is to Pray—True Gentility—Beginning at the Bottom—The Pottery District—Mr. Wedgwood—Progress in the Art of Pottery—Enterprise and Success—Honour and Emolument—The True Workman—The Ornamental and the Useful—Union of both : Hence Success—Gratifying Testimonials—An Urgent Want—Supply and Demand—Great Manufacturing Centres—Masters and Men, their Mutual Relations—A Pattern Master honoured in his Workpeople—The True Directory, studied and observed—A Critical Position Skilfully Mastered—The Friend in the Master—Open Profession—Its peculiar Responsibilities—Light Shining—One in Christ—An Offending Brother—The Brother Gained—The Wisdom from Beneath—The Wisdom from Above ....*Page* 37

CHAPTER IV.

THE ELDER OF THE CHURCH.

The Fire Kindled—The Fire Spreading—The Day of Small Things—Increase and Strength—Strength claiming acknowledgment—Trouble resulting therefrom—Complaint and Petition—Frustration of Hopes—Beginning again—First Impressions—Fireside Conferences—A Touching Incident—The Pledge Redeemed—A Twofold Lesson improved—Constitutions must grow—Conflict and Labour—Experience Gained—Office of Ruling Elder—Reasons for the Office—The Prince of Delegates—Business a Pleasure—Methodical in Habit—Persistent in Effort—Fluent in Speech—Strong in Conviction—Skilful in Debate—Hasty in Temper—Reconcilable and Reconciling in Spirit—Acquired Influence—Benefits Conferred—A Connexional Desideratum; Efforts to supply it—
—Opposition overcome—The "Apology," &c.—Authorship—A Crucial Test—Shipwreck of Faith—The Descent easy, after the first step—The Corrupt Branch cut off—Loss and Gain—Sacrifices and Labours—Manifold services of Mr. Ridgway—Public Religious Meetings—Religious Societies—Chairmanship—Ability and Adaptability—Grave and Gay—Kindly Humour—Smiles and Tears .... *Page* 77

CHAPTER V.

THE LABOURER IN THE VINEYARD.

Piety rather than Partisanship—A Trinity of Duties—The Strait Gate made straiter—Christian Catholicity—Caring most for one's own—Every Talent used—Recruiting for Christ—Clerical, yet not Clerical—A Word fitly spoken—Characteristics of Preaching—Duty of Prayer—Its seasonableness and advantage—The Sign and the thing signified—The Redeemer and His Work—Wayside Hearers—Unproductive Soil—Fruit to Eternal Life—Private Ministry—The Early Summons—Counsels and Consolations—More than a Conqueror—Sorrow lightened by Sympathy—After the fathers the children ...*Page* 141

CHAPTER VI.

UNCONSCIOUS SELF-PORTRAITURE.

A Man's True Self—Voices from Within—Transitory Glimpses—Character of Diary—Adieu to Home—Out at Sea—Still Busy—Outgoings of the Morning—Labour and Profit—Absent yet Present—The Capital of New England—The Pearl of Days—The Joy of Worship—A Musical Performance—Business fairly begun—An Educational establishment—Course of Instruction—Supported by the State—Practical interest in Education—Visit to the States' Gaol—Employment of Prisoners—Day of Rest—A Weak Vessel—White and Black—The Bostonians—Their Faith—Their Politics—Still Onward—Notes by the Way—Sabbath Experiences—Philadelphian Prison—Bettering House—An Exemplary Spirit—Two Memorable Events—Penance rather than Profit—Homeward Bound—Sunshine and Shade—Regret and Resolution—Now and Then—The Empire City—England, with all thy faults, &c.—English love of Home—Jubilant, yet Prayerful—Again on the Deep—Christmas Day—Self-Communings—Delay and Disappointment—An Ebenezer raised at Sea—An Agreeable Surprise—Home, sweet Home......... *Page* 173

CHAPTER VII.

POLITICS AND PHILANTHROPY.

Beauty of Holiness—Sympathy with Suffering—A Sermon without Words—A Philanthropist of noble type—Philanthropy practical and particular—The True Neighbour—Doing good by stealth—Always Giving—From Philanthropy to Politics—Conservatism and Progress—An Arena of Dust and Danger—Political Leadership—The Reform Bill—Public excitement—Speech at a County Meeting—The Bill, the whole Bill, and nothing but the Bill—Reasons for Reform—Encouragements—Wise but Resolute Counsels—Loyalty with Liberalism—Age of Chivalry not Past—An Englishman Abroad—Many Irons in the Fire—Smiles for Home—Work Self-rewarding—Pains and Penalties—Civil Honours worthily bestowed—A distinction declined—The reason why—The noblest Recompenses—Others in their train .... *Page* 231

CHAPTER VIII.

THE FAITH KEPT, THE COURSE FINISHED.

A Green Old Age—The Crown of Old Men—A Hearth not Lonely, nor Sad—Love Given and Returned—A Life beautiful and blessed—One taken, the other left—Sorrowful, yet Rejoicing—The Great Refuge—Christian Submission—Christian Anticipation—Vigorous Health—The Best not the Beginning—Not yet venerable—A Dreary Prospect—Sanctified Affliction—Ripening for the Harvest—A Noble Maxim—Less for the World—Enough and to Spare—Not by Bread alone—Source of Real Enjoyment—Death before the Time—More for the Church—Nearness to Heaven—Concern for Sinners—Means to save them—Craving for visible success—A Characteristic not too common—Employment of Leisure—The Last Work done—Good Night—Then Rest—Sudden Death, Sudden Glory—A Town in Mourning—The Living honouring the Dead—Impressive Ceremonial—A Solemn Farewell—A Standard-bearer Fallen—The Dead in Christ blessed—They Rest from their Labours—And their Works do follow them—Lessons to be learnt—Wisdom the principal thing—The Common Lot—The Lighted Valley—Hear us, good Lord. *Page* 269

CHAPTER I.

Eminent Men Centres of Historic Interest.

CHAPTER I.

EMINENT MEN CENTRES OF HISTORIC INTEREST.

History, it is said, is philosophy teaching by example. But the example must be that of individual men, if the philosophy is that of human thought and motive. Biography, then, is the proper sphere of this—is certainly that department of history in which the particular instruction most abounds. This takes us upward to the very springs of action, and downward in their after flow, as the springs widen into streams. It reveals the play and counter-play of the several faculties, according to their native tendencies, in the struggle after inward or outward good; the silent growth of the mind under the culture it receives, and its subsequent outgrowth into the particular habits and pursuits which definitely attest its character. True of biography in general, this is especially true of the biographies of remarkable men. History, indeed, is very much made up of such biographies; if not formally, yet virtually and in fact: while there are many remarkable men of whom history, as well from its ordinary plan as from the necessity of selection imposed upon it, can take but little account.

This applies to *written* history. In *actual* history no one is lost,—no single individual counts for nothing. The impression he makes may be slight, scarcely perceptible—a mere ripple on the surface, appearing soon to subside—but it is, nevertheless, real, and may possibly swell, though we see it not, in wave upon wave for ever. A man must have an influence proportioned to the sum of his being, to the power he possesses and actively puts forth. Where this power is great, the influence also will be great; and hence the reason for the statement sometimes made, that the history of society is the history of its great men.

This seems to imply that society takes its mould from these; that the activities and general complexion of society at particular periods are very much determined by one or more superior minds which rule over it with a kingly sway. But there is another theory, the opposite of this, which makes such minds, at least in what they accomplish, the product—if I may so speak—of the generation to which they belong. The truth is, no exclusive theory can be established, while each of these views may be maintained on the special ground chosen by its advocates, with a force of reasoning to which there can hardly be any reply. The occasion makes the man, it is said; but it may be also said that the man makes the occasion. The former saying, if taken absolutely, would go far to destroy human freedom; the latter, if considered alone, would do much to exclude the idea of a presiding Providence and a definite plan. Each gives but the half of a whole, and both together are required to express one complete truth.

There is, in the general play of kindred forces, a reciprocal operation. We have impression and rebound, action and reaction. Circumstances do much for a man; but he is a poor specimen of his race who is only just what circumstances make him. He resigns his personality, and becomes himself a circumstance. While no one is independent of outward conditions, while outward conditions have considerable effect upon us, no one becomes really great who has not first the greatness in himself. A truly great man gathers up into the substance of his own character whatever will give him nurture or stimulus, and then becomes a centre from which to radiate the heat and reflect the light which he himself has received. He attracts to himself the elements and influences that are at work about him, blindly struggling towards an end that is felt rather than seen; gives them in his own purpose a direction, and in his own speech a language; and thereby operates with mighty impression upon masses that come to acknowledge him as chief.

But then he has the power to do this—the capacity to receive, the will to execute—or the work could not be done. The like achievement would be impossible to a man of less original capability. Luther, no doubt, had been anticipated and prepared for, in what had occurred before him. The age was ripe for his appearance; Christendom waited for him. He came into possession of a rich inheritance of circumstances favourable to the work he was to do. But it was a Luther for whom the preparation was made. No other could have answered the call of the times, or have been the interpreter of the needs of the Church. One such as he was required to make his own the position that was to be occupied, to turn to adequate account the opportunities that were fast accumulating, to execute the high commission which Providence was plainly giving to some one. So, at a later period, the same state of things appealed in the very same language to many good men at the same time; the like circumstances were ready to mould them to heroic stature, and to inspire them with more than heroic ardour; but it was reserved for Wesley—because, in fact, Wesley was in himself the most fitting instrument for this—to become the leader of a movement which, while rousing from its torpor the religious life of a whole nation, was destined to result in one of the most stupendous organizations for the diffusion of Christianity which the Church of Christ has ever known.

Now, it is the achievements of such men that furnish the material of history. Sometimes, indeed, of men inferior to these, even though history should not mention their names; while, again, it is the lives of such that abound in the example by which philosophy is said to be taught. There is hardly any exercise more useful than the study of these. They make the past live before us. They bring us into the presence of men of whom the world was not worthy. They reveal to us their inner and their outer life; make us companions of their course, observers of what they think and do. They show the power of thought, the force of will, the supremacy of conscience. They illustrate the beauty and blessedness of holy living, the positive advantage in the long run, notwithstanding the apparent confusion of things, of all that our higher judgments pronounce to be true and good. They indicate the laws of human progress, marking step by step the onward march of civilization and religion; teach us what, by the utmost stretch of his capacity, is possible to man, and what, though not at the time possible, it is, nevertheless, noble to aim at.

Methodism is richer in nothing than in its biographies. It has now lived long enough to have many of these. Great names are not wanting to it—names which the world will not willingly let die. Great memories are a part of the inheritance it transmits to its children. Literature and scholarship are both worthily represented in its history; especially considering the comparative recency of its origin, and the work which, by distinct preference, it has set itself to do. In the article of literature, indeed, even this qualification need not be made, particularly if the view be confined to that class of writings whose object it is to foster the growth of personal piety and zeal, and to preserve and to spread the faith which was once delivered to the saints. So of the power—than which there are few higher powers—of organization and government; the power which combines individual elements into one orderly mass, and makes them as a single agency—" moving altogether when it moves at all"—for the accomplishment of some great and definite purpose. Few communities can compare with Methodism in examples of this power, the great and definite purpose in its case being the furtherance of the Gospel both at home and abroad.

But, as indeed the last remark implies, Methodism is distinctively, as it is professedly, an aggressive form of Christianity. A high authority has pronounced it "Christianity in earnest." It came into existence when there was pressing need of it, else it had not been; a need then but little recognised, though now universally acknowledged. It was raised up to reanimate a dying creed, and make it the symbol of a living faith; to trim and rekindle the lamps that were growing dim in the sanctuary, that the way into the Holiest might not be missed; to carry their light abroad, beyond the precincts of the sanctuary, even though, as in the case of Gideon's army, in "empty pitchers," that the multitudes of our countrymen who sat in the region and shadow of death might at least catch one ray of it; to make religion, where it was professed, but only too little known, a thing of life and power—a joy, in fact, to millions, dead, living, or yet to be born. Its memories, therefore, are for the most part those of sainted piety and of ministerial efficiency; of faith before which mountains disappeared; of zeal that many waters could not quench; of love that wept to see others weep, and dried its tears in drying theirs. Its biographies are those of Christian men, of men made Christian through its means; not seldom of men in humble life, whom, nevertheless, God will reckon among the choicest of His jewels, in that day when He shall make them up; sometimes of men who, by the native force of their character, and the sanctification of the Holy Spirit, have pressed their way upward and onward through a crowd of obstructions, until, as ministers of the Gospel, they have shone like stars in the right hand of the Son of God; often of men who, under its shadow and fostering nurture, have risen to affluence, to high positions, to commanding influence, to great usefulness in almost every department of human labour.

It is one of this last description, and one occupying a foremost place in the class to which he belonged, whose history and character we have now to sketch. Our sketch may fail to present him as he really was, but it will serve to vivify the recollections of those who knew him, and it may be to profit, if not by instruction, yet by stimulus, those who knew him not. It *must* in detail be less complete than we could wish: partly because such a life as his leaves little for the biographer but a series of public and private acts of similar kind, which, though it were noble to perform, it would be tedious or ostentatious to repeat; partly because this little is rendered still less for our purpose by the absence of memoranda which he alone could have furnished, but which he was ever too busy to make; and partly, again, because many facts and incidents which in other men's lives would be deemed remarkable, were in his scarcely observed, or with only the impression of the passing moment, seeing they were not exceptional or peculiar, but fell harmoniously in with a life of which the whole key was above the common pitch. But whatever the deficiency of our portrait—however it may fail in breadth or minuteness, in likeness or in finish—it will assuredly be the portrait of one who was thought of while living, and will long be remembered, now dead, as a PRINCE IN ISRAEL.

CHAPTER II.

Natural Endowments and Home Influences.

CHAPTER II.

NATURAL ENDOWMENTS AND HOME INFLUENCES.

John Ridgway was born at Hanley, Staffordshire Potteries, on the 1st of February, 1786. He died there, at Cauldon Place, nearly seventy-five years after. He thus survived the ordinary term of human life, coming close upon the period when man's strength is said to be labour and sorrow. Labour and sorrow it might have been to him, had he been spared till then; but there was less in his case to foreshadow this experience than in the case of most who live as long as he. In him life was vigorous to the last—so vigorous, that it might almost be said of him, as was said of Moses, whose death, like his own, was but just a retirement from labour, "his eye was not dim, nor his natural force abated."

"Whom the gods love die young," was a saying

of the ancient heathen. The sentiment is pleasing, and not without a certain element of truth. We have the same feeling ourselves, when a child of rare endowment, of strange wisdom and sweetness, is taken away from us. Not seldom, also, in view of the evils that are thereby avoided and of the blessedness that is thereby insured, we speak of it as a happy thing for children to die young. And happy it certainly is, since the covenant of redeeming mercy has made it so: for of such is the kingdom of heaven. But it is far more happy to live long and well, to live laboriously and usefully, to achieve much for oneself and still more for others, thus to become, in the language of the prophet, "an old man that hath filled his days"; and then, like fruit full grown and ripe, to fall without violence into the hands of the great husbandman, when in due season he comes to gather and to garner. So lived and so died John Ridgway.

A character like his is no accident, nor is it of human fabrication merely. No character is, though in some there is infinitely more of purpose and of training than in others. Nor is it wholly a growth, unless by growth be meant the development under wise and patient nurture of that which has great original capability. So considered, it *is* a growth; and this, perhaps, gives us the correctest view of it. It is like a plant of noble stock, or rather germ of the rarer sort, which, because cultivated by a skilful hand and with watchful tenderness, shoots steadily up into leafy luxuriance and solid strength of stem and branch, and, when the time comes, rewards the care bestowed upon it by a plentiful crop of goodly fruit. Character in general, indeed, as well as that character which claims attention by its special excellence, depends much upon the same conditions; first upon what is natural to man, and then upon the kind of education he receives.

In both these Mr. Ridgway was singularly favoured. What he had from nature was, if not of the best, yet very high in the comparison with ordinary endowments. He had a strong physical constitution; marked in feature, and, in matured life, massive in build. Inheriting this at birth, he never lost it: so that he knew little of sickness, and not much more of fatigue. His perpetual health kept him perpetually cheerful, ever able to work, and ever delighting in work. Life in him was nothing feeble, nothing sluggish, but of tidal strength and freshness, coursing with deep and rapid current through all the channels where life could circulate or throb.

His mind was not unsuited to its dwelling-place. There was, in fact, an admirable fitness and adjustment in the two; the one corresponding to the other, as if on some principle of pre-established harmony. It may be that this is always the case, or with only rare exceptions, that the body is a fitting instrument, as also a fitting expression of the mind: so that if one were skilled in such mysteries, were keen-sighted enough to decipher the language of material signs, it would be easy—far more easy than by observing certain prominences and depressions on the skull—to arrive at some probable judgment concerning man's natural character by means of outward form and feature. It cannot be but that the mind has much to do with the moulding of the body, as it has certainly much to do with its use and destiny; not, however, as the embryo of it, nor as identical with the principle which we call life, but still as something vital and penetrative—a force ever present and ever operative, refining or debasing, exalting or humbling, as its own nature may be. In this respect we claim for Mr. Ridgway nothing very extraordinary. Intellectually considered, his powers were not of the highest order: they were yet such as gave him no great difficulty in mastering what he was wishful to understand. Sagacity, shrewdness, humour, wit, with an ardent temperament, great good-nature, and an instinct that turned everything to some practical account—these were among his most observable characteristics; and these were purely natural. Whatever that quality may be which we denominate "common sense," which we claim as a specially distinctive feature of the English mind, and which no training will effectually give, he possessed in a high degree. Power he had, whatever is meant by that term; and this apart from the mere influence of acquired position. It was power innate and personal, becoming in effect the power of mind over mind, and of one mind over many minds. Probably this power was the property of no faculty in particular, but was the result of the whole sum of his faculties, which, while there was nothing very remarkable in any one, were in their general substance and combination a much more than common endowment.

With superior natural gifts, he had, to begin with, a happy home and a thoroughly Christian education. These are peculiar advantages, in the absence of which the highest gifts may be the heaviest misfortunes. A happy home is the nursery of the sweetest charities; a Christian education is the means to the noblest virtues. "Whose are the fathers," says the apostle, in giving an inventory of the great and distinguishing privileges of the ancient Jews; from which a learned writer thus beautifully discourses: "Nobility is commonly held in the highest esteem. But a true nobility consists not in having descended from a line of kings, but in having for our fathers and grandfathers those who were the children of God; in being so trained and nurtured at home, that piety is taken in with our mother's milk; and in receiving from our parents the blessing assured in the Divine promise, 'I will be a God unto thee, and to thy seed after thee.'"*

So Cowper sweetly sings—

> "My boast is not that I deduce my birth
> From loins enthroned, and rulers of the earth;
> But higher far my proud pretensions rise,—
> The son of parents pass'd into the skies."

Mr. Ridgway belonged to what is called a good family, though it is difficult with certainty to trace its genealogy far backward.† He was the eldest

---

* Cocceius. The words are worth quoting in the original: "Nobilitas pro maxime æstimatur in seculo. Non est vera nobilitas, atavis editum esse regibus; sed patres et avos habere filios Dei, atque ita domesticam et familiarem habere pietatem, verbum pietatis cum lacte materna hausisse, et a parentibus benedictionem accepisse, subnixam divina promissione, *Ero Deus tuus et seminis tui post te.*"

† I have before me several documents, apparently preserved with great care, which seem to have been drawn up and collected with a view to connect the family, in one line of descent, with a family which began to be of some consequence as early as the time of Edward the Fourth. This family was settled in Devonshire, "in the neighbourhood of Tor Abbey, in the church of which there are several monuments (of the family), and near it a large extent of ground, still called Ridgway plains." Some of the members served in important civil

son of Job Ridgway, one of the eminent potters who acquired reputation and wealth towards the close of the last and the beginning of the present century. Of the father, we learn something from his own pen, and something more from the pen of his son, whose joint contributions were published in a short memoir soon after his death. In this memoir we are told that the grandfather " possessed a very good estate;" but, being thoughtless and dissipated, soon involved himself in trouble, and in the end was compelled to work for a living. This also was the necessity of Job, and at a very early period; but with this difference of result, that by working he redeemed the fortunes of his family, in becoming a successful and comparatively wealthy manufacturer.

This result was doubtless aided by a character greatly different from that of his father; different, at least, from his twenty-first year, for at that

---

capacities, and even won distinction. Of these was John Ridgway, Member of Parliament for Exeter in the reign of Mary, of whom one of the said monuments reports, that he was "a man of good and liberal education, well versed in transacting affairs, and deserving well of his country for his fidelity to Henry the Eighth, Edward the Sixth, and Queen Mary." Another, Thomas Ridgway, was knighted; and a third was ennobled, though the title afterwards became extinct. One branch of the family removed into Cheshire some time during the seventeenth century; and it was with this that Mr. Ridgway was connected, if connected with the family at all.

time he became openly and decidedly a follower of Christ. His conversion was marked and complete, shedding the influence of grace on his whole subsequent life. He had previously known the bitterness of sin—in many a struggle with the lust of his own heart, in many a conflict with the enticements of the world; but now his pain rose to agony, and his agony, like the darkness that precedes the dawn, was the virtual harbinger of most heavenly peace. While at prayer, as he himself tells us, his soul "entered into rest;" and his language was, "Come and hear, all ye that fear God, and I will declare what He hath done for my soul." He did declare, and the declaration resulted, in a few months, in the conversion of about twenty-five others. His religious life partook of the energy that was natural to him, and this was sufficient to carry him into any enterprise which wisdom or piety could suggest or justify. The force of his regenerated character soon made itself felt on all about him—in the church, at the manufactory, pre-eminently at home, everywhere — appearing ever in new forms of activity, as new relations were entered into, or as new duties, or a more extended sphere of them, arose out of more prosperous circumstances. With a loving remembrance of his virtues, the son, dwelling on each with a fond minuteness of detail, tells what he was and what he did in almost every private and public relation; how that, as a member of civil society, he loved his country, and withheld his hand from nothing that he could do to promote the common good; how that, as a worshipper in the house of God, he was always, whoever might officiate, and whatever the state of the weather, among the first and most regular there, giving also to those in his employment the same opportunity to attend the week-night service as he himself enjoyed; how that, as one engaged occasionally in the ministry of the Gospel, he had an intimate acquaintance with Divine truth, and so proclaimed it that few in the like circumstances were rendered so great a blessing as he; how that, in yet another office, that of class-leader, his efficiency was such that the church was greatly enlarged by his exertions; how that, finally, and more particularly for our purpose, having himself "a singular depth and clearness of religious experience, and a close communion with God through the Spirit," he sought, as the head of a family, like Abraham, to "command his children and his household after him," took a peculiar delight in reading the Word of God, or in hearing it read, and had so sacred a regard to morning and evening devotion, that not a single omission of family prayer at these times was ever known to have taken place.

With a wife likeminded, as his wife was,—loved with tender esteem, and worthy to be so loved: meet companion and help in all domestic duties and joys: having the same desires and the same aims: caring much, it may be, though not unwisely, for the temporal well-being of their children, but much more, most anxiously in fact, for their nurture in the Lord,—what a bright, blessed home, what a nursery—warm, sheltered, sunny—for the early quickening and growth of plants one day to become trees of righteousness, must theirs have been! That it was so is evidenced by many testimonies, not least by the keen sorrow and sense of bereavement with which, as parents, their death was mourned, together with the loving recollections that ever afterwards spontaneously sprang up on the mention of their names; still more in the fact that their children while young became devoutly religious, placing themselves under the spiritual oversight of their father as a leader in the church, and only cleaving with the attachment of a stronger faith to the things which they had learnt from him, the more seducing the temptation, from increasing worldly prosperity, to unlearn or forget them.

Of John we have it distinctly on record—he often affirmed it himself—that he inhaled the spirit of piety within the charmed circle of his childhood's home. The atmosphere of Christianity was the atmosphere into which he was born. Not only from what we know of the character of his parents does this appear, but also from a specific memorandum of his father, in which, speaking for himself and his wife, he says, "The year following," that is, their marriage, "the Lord gave us a son, and we considered it a pledge of His kindness: we called his name John." What was received as from the Lord, was thought of as belonging to Him. The atmosphere into which this son came ever surrounded him, for the thought that he was the Lord's was never surrendered and never forgotten. He breathed it continually; unconsciously of course at first, but even then, it may be, not without some spiritual advantage; afterwards by free choice and with positive delight, as an atmosphere which had in a certain sense become natural to him. Hence it might be said of him, though with due reverence and a full appreciation of the difference that must exist between the "holy child Jesus" and any other child, "The child grew, and waxed strong in spirit, filled with wisdom: and the grace of God was upon him."

It is not meant by this that, as a boy, John Ridgway was wholly unlike all other boys, and therefore, in fact, not a boy; that he was ever correct and regular, demanding no oversight, and giving no one any trouble; that he thought nothing of play, but much of books; and was always innocent of joke, and frolic, and laughter. Who then would have liked him? A melancholy picture is that which Wordsworth gives, in the lines—

> "Her infant babe
> Had from his mother caught the trick of grief,
> And sighed among its playthings."

And what can be less lovely than a child that is ever grave and precise, without the sportive mirth, and winsome ways, and guileless irregularities of a heart that rejoices, just as the bird sings, it knows not why, and never cares to inquire? Such a conception would ill accord with what we know of Mr. Ridgway as a man. He was buoyant as a lark that tosses the morning dew from its wings; had ever a cheerful spirit to lean against every adverse wind; was full of gaiety and humour in the presence of friends—sometimes carrying these to the very verge of license; yet tender withal, moved to tears as readily as to laughter—for, in truth, humour and pathos are twin sisters, and seldom live apart.

"He was cheerful and good-humoured, full of spirit and energy, fond of joke and fun, and always a peacemaker. . . . . . Altogether he was a fine, frank, open English lad, and a favourite with both master and boys." So testifies one who knew him at school; and we must have believed it, though no such testimony had been borne. We can picture him only as a bright, cheery boy, with clear expansive forehead, crowned and curtained with light clustering hair; a mouth round and full, set continually for speech; an eye small, but observant, twinkling ever with a sly, genial humour; a whole countenance, in fact, radiant as sunbeams, and which, though liable in certain electric conditions to be overcast and stormy, is ready at any moment to break into ripples of guileless and good-natured merriment. We can think of him, and must think of him, as ever busy and buoyant, giving much concern to those about him, by his troublesome playfulness and propensity for mischief, yet disarming their anger by the arch expression of his rosy countenance, and the musical ring of his merry laugh; as ready for every kind of sport, and rushing eagerly into it, though less from any desire to excel than as finding pleasure in the bare excitement; as giving Mr. Kemp, his first schoolmaster at Burslem, and the Rev. Mr. Truman, a Baptist minister in Leicestershire, under whom he was subsequently placed, no little trouble by his exuberant gaiety and fondness for amusement and adventure,—proving by his roguish disregard of small proprieties more attractive to the class than was the book to be conned, and making, for the time, the lesson somewhat difficult to learn; yet still, and in spite of all this, as the above witness deponeth, "a favourite with both master and boys,"—with boys for his natural frankness and generous peace-loving disposition, which made him, while averse to enmities, not cowardly in the maintenance of right,—with masters for the like qualities, and for others not now so perceptible, perhaps, but to be developed in some serviceable way in a yet unknown future.

Tenderly did he love his mother, as tenderly she deserved to be loved; but this did not prevent him from giving her perpetual anxiety, especially when out of her sight, by his impulsive energy, and heedless pursuit of whatever his fancy inclined to. Nor was her anxiety without reason, for his buoyant spirit, his fulness of passionate life, took little account of danger; and danger was often so near as seemingly to make death not very distant.

In one instance of this there was something of the ludicrous, though doubtless, at the time, sufficient of the alarming. His brother and himself were playing in the Hanley Market, the shambles of which were moveable stalls. On these stalls, against all remonstrance and clear prophecy of coming trouble, master John must climb; and not only climb, but choose them for sundry exercises in a gymnastique peculiarly his own. There might be danger, but there was also sport. Sport and not danger was what the lad wanted. So he closed his eye to one, and opened it to the other. He got both, with some damage, and a fortunate deliverance. In the middle of one of his spirited evolutions he tripped, lost his balance, dropped between two stalls, and hung suspended on a hook through the ear.

Not long after this, the two brothers were passing down a road in the neighbourhood of Hanley, close to which colliery operations had formerly been carried on. Out of the shaft of a coal-pit, now disused, a martin took wing. What boy ever denied himself the privilege of looking for a bird's-nest where the spring of a bird gave promise of its accessible presence? This was certainly a privilege not to be sacrificed by the elder of these brothers, particularly if it could be spiced and made piquant by difficulty or peril in the attainment of it. In this case it might be, as there were both these stimulants. The shaft rose high above the level of the road, and had been so long out of use, that the masonry had given way, and a rank vegetation had treacherously encircled the pit's mouth. Up John scrambled, tearing his way to the brink, heedless again of admonition and warning. After him sped his brother, though at cautious and measured distance; still near, because apprehensive of all but certain disaster. Across the deceitful parapet the boy, thinking only of his prize, impatiently stretched himself. Down went the bricks, and down must himself have gone too, but that his brother caught his tilting heels, and restored for a moment his lost equilibrium. But only for a moment, for other bricks in the faithless wall followed the former, snatching back the recovered odds against the poor child's life. Frantic with fear, the boys struggled, the elder all but impotent, the younger strong above his natural strength by the terror that inspired him. As one sank within, the other purposely sank without, thus increasing the leverage, on the maintenance of which a life held dear at home now wholly hung. Seconds passed, hardly seconds; the grip was tightened, the swaying wall stood firm, and the too ardent student of natural history found himself, by one desperate effort, redeemed from a violent death. Of this escapade, the mother (for to her the thought instantly turned) was to know nothing; and, accordingly, nothing was told her.

Out of this adventure grew caution—a little, and only for a season; or not enough or long enough to prevent similar adventures, with similar dangers and deliverances. He must mount a horse which he could not manage, not doubting of his ability, however—for he was fond of riding—or rather, perhaps, not thinking of ability at all. He had the not uncommon reward of such rashness, though in a degree uncommonly severe. He was taken up by his father from a fall as one that was dead; and afterwards rode with too vivid a remembrance of his misfortune ever to ride well. He must bathe in the Trent, at a bend of the river where the water was pounded for the use of a mill hard by. The water was deep; he knew not how deep. The sloping bank had been eaten away by the sweep of the current, so that he could not wade. Nor did he wish to wade. He wanted a plunge, though he could not swim. His companions—of whom there were two—less impetuous than he, were slower in their preparations. Ready first, in he went, replying to their entreaties to wait, by a careless, "Oh, I can manage;" but he managed so ill that he could find no bottom, and soon lost sight of the top; sank, and sank again, and was on the point of sinking for ever, when rescue came by the hands of his two companions, both relatives, who ventured their own lives to save his.

The last two instances occurred at a period somewhat later than the one at which, as yet, we are supposed to have arrived. They are inserted here, however, because they fall in with and continue that view of Mr. Ridgway's youthful character which is now more particularly under notice; also, to avoid the necessity of any future reference to them, or to what they may be supposed to illustrate. Other instances, not less remarkable, more so, indeed, transpired in Mr. Ridgway's subsequent history; but these were referrible in no ascertainable degree to the same personal qualities which seem to have given rise to those recorded above. They were rather occurrences which thoughtfulness usually denominates accidents, fortunate escapes, &c., but which piety delights to think of, and in fact instinctively recognises, as dangers and deliverances connected in some way with an ever-watchful and all-embracing Providence. Nor should we be safe in severing this same Providence from our view of those events in early life which, as to their immediate origin, may be safely put down to an ardour of temperament which only experience and the discipline of years could turn to profitable account. The whole meaning of such events is not explained when we have catalogued the attendant circumstances, and traced their visible connexion. We know, as a matter of fact, that Joseph and Mary were directed by the angel of the Lord to flee with the infant Jesus into Egypt; but what if nothing had been recorded but the flight itself? Could we have regarded the escape of the child from the wrath of Herod as otherwise than intensely providential? In other senses than the one intended by the poet—in the sense of watchful oversight and invisible protection and guidance—

" Heaven lies about our infancy."

It was an occurrence which Mr. Ridgway laid wholly to the account of a providence, which in his life had often been special, that, on his return from the Paris Exhibition, in 1855, stepping into a railway carriage at Dover, and by some means falling headlong between the wheels and the platform, just as the train was about to move, he was taken up without having sustained any material injury. This deliverance was mentioned with tears, and ever afterwards thought of with thankfulness. Some men's lives abound in such; Mr. Ridgway's was one.

"Think first," is doubtless sage advice; but to take it requires the habit to have been already formed. It certainly demands a larger experience, or a completer balance of faculties, than boys usually possess. It is sufficient for them to feel, and feeling is to them the motive for action. They hence act first, and think after: but by this means they come in time—if they come to anything of worth—to think first, and act after. Especially is this the case with such boys as the subject of our narrative. They are carried out and carried away by the ardour of their temperament, but not for this reason necessarily carried into evil. Sin resides not in the temperament, but in the affections and the will. The ardour itself is good, a constitutional endowment of great practical utility. True, in a man who has lived and learnt nothing, it may become a sign of weakness, as indicating the confirmed supremacy of mere feeling over judgment; but, in a boy, it is, or may be, that rude, undisciplined force, which in after life is secretly transformed into manly purpose and noble enterprise—that vital energy, impulsive and unreasoning in its own nature, but which, under chosen regulations of a growing wisdom and the manifold corrections of ripening experience, glorifies itself in a variety of achievement and result, of which, while the visible monuments are in this world, the more enduring record is on high.

CHAPTER III.

The Successful Manufacturer.

CHAPTER III.

THE SUCCESSFUL MANUFACTURER.

In the foregoing chapter we have obtained a glimpse of John Ridgway at school, but only a glimpse, for nothing more is permitted us. Probably, a closer inspection would yield but little worth recording, as school-days are very much the same to all, differing mainly in this, that one has greater advantages than another, or uses to a greater profit such as he has.

Of some who acquire distinction, it is the delight of biographers to tell how marvellously clever they were in youth; of others, how marvellously dull. And doubtless both qualities are met with; as in boys generally, so in that select number of them who in after life become "from their shoulders and upward higher than any of the people;" for minds, like plants, do not all bloom at the same age, or in conditions of culture precisely similar. Of John Ridgway neither of these things could be said. He was neither precocious nor stupid; but, says one who knew him at school, and whose testimony on another point has been already given, "of fair average ability;" or, as a second says, unless this second is the first in other words, "of a lively, happy disposition, and quick in learning his lessons." Quickness in learning lessons is perfectly consistent with what is deemed a fair average ability, particularly when, as in his case, the lessons are no great trial of intellectual capacity. He was no doubt educated with care, and as certainly with wisdom too. His home education was of the best which our choicest English homes can boast of. The most competent schoolmaster in the neighbourhood was chosen to supplement the instruction given him in his father's house; and when it was deemed advisable to give him other advantages than he had yet enjoyed, he was placed under a godly minister in another county, that heart, and head, and outward life might all be under due training at the same time. Still, though his education was conducted with care, it was conducted without pretension and without ambition. No intellectual eminence was sought for him, as probably none was desired by him. He was hence subjected to no particular drill, beyond that required for an ordinary commercial education of the better class; and this being gone through with a completeness deemed sufficient in his case at the termination of his fifteenth year, he was at that age taken from school altogether.

From school to business he was taken. This is the natural order, where order can be observed at all, though the business may be as varied as human tastes or as human wants. Few are born above the necessity of labour—none above the duty; none therefore really above the necessity, in the larger and higher meaning of the term. Manual labour is only one of many kinds of labour that may be chosen or must be accepted, and not necessarily the most toilsome or trying one. It is not, if we may believe one whose experience certainly qualified him to judge,* even the least favourable to intellectual culture, or, what is more, to successful authorship; the proof of this lying broadly in the fact, which himself indeed is careful to point out, that the class to which the ploughman and the operative mechanic belong is better represented in our literature than are some other classes of genteeler occupation. But, however this may be, certain it is that work is multitudinous in its kinds, and that to work is the

* Hugh Miller. *My Schools and Schoolmasters.*

appointed destiny of man. Not his misfortune, though, much less his punishment. Labour is not the infliction of justice, but the ordination of benevolence. "To dress and to keep it," man was originally placed in Paradise. If this were a garden prepared for him, it was also a garden to be kept by him: to be kept as a garden, and not allowed to grow into a wilderness—its endless varieties of mingling beauty blooming under his eye, not by miracle, but by means of his ever-patient skill; its continually changing harvests of fruit and food coming to perfection for his use, not irrespectively of his care, but by the most assiduous though cheerful industry, the labours of his hands keeping stroke to the chime of his grateful affections; the whole thus contributing to his enjoyment, not by a single element, but by the twofold satisfaction of seeing in the one result both the bounty of his Creator and the reward of his own work.

Not till sin entered did work lose its sacredness or its joy. It then became a toil, a weariness, a sorrow—something to be done in the sweat of the face, and something to be done for daily bread. It is so now; but chiefly as sin makes it so. Wherever sin mingles with it, or is connected with it—in the sense of indolence, love of ease, vanity, pride, selfishness—there is hardship in it.

Sin makes it bitter as a task, though at the same time not unserviceable for discipline, or unavailing as punishment. But in itself, work is still honourable. In all real work there is dignity, as in all there is profit. Wherever the heart directs the hands, and desire gives energy to the will,—where the work is chosen wisely, or, if not chosen, yet performed cheerfully, as a service of duty, and means in some way of good,—it is true now as of old, and must be true for ever, that "to labour is to pray."

Error on this point is far from rare, infesting almost every class of society. An outward show of respectability is far more coveted than honest industry. The man whom Providence has so favoured that he has no need to labour in order to live, is commonly, and very much for that reason, called a gentleman. So also is the man who, though not thus favoured, yet contrives somehow to live on other people's labours. Work is thus virtually opposed to worth; at least, it is thought of as something which degrades, rather than as something which ennobles. This is especially true of the work which taxes the limbs, or soils the clothes.

Now nothing can be more false, and nothing more mischievous. It is important for all classes to rid themselves of a notion so utterly wrong, that the highest may learn to work as a duty, and the lowest to be gentle as the best. Neither fortune nor position can make a gentleman, nor can utmost poverty unmake him, when once made. Gentility, as a rule, may have something to do with race, or rather with high physical conditions, occasioned partly by comparative pureness of descent; but as it is eminently mental and moral, it consists mainly in that which can be acquired by discipline and culture, marking itself generally in a refinement of sensibility which is readily susceptible of outward impressions, and in a *goodness* of behaviour which springs immediately and naturally out of true goodness of heart. Goodness is at the bottom of it all, as this is the root from which germinate and blossom,—whether with wild freedom or with trained exactness,—the delicate courtesies and self-forgetting sympathies which alone can entitle a man to be considered gentle. An aversion to labour can never do this, much less can a contempt for it. It is almost sure to do precisely the opposite; while, on the other hand, the humblest work which a man can do, and which under the pressure of the most grinding necessity he is compelled to do, need not prevent in him the cultivation of those qualities which, in all but their visible polish, would pass for the virtues of a true and noble gentleness.

Very well worth quoting in this connexion are the words of one of our greatest living writers. "Gentlemen," says Mr. Ruskin, "have to learn that it is no part of their duty or privilege to live on other people's toil. They have to learn that there is no degradation in the hardest manual, or the humblest servile labour, when it is needed. But that there *is* degradation, and that deep, in extravagance, in bribery, in indolence, in pride, in taking places that they are not fit for, or in coining places for which there is no need. It does not disgrace a gentleman to become an errand-boy or a day labourer; but it disgraces much to become a knave or a thief. And knavery is not the less knavery because it involves large interests, nor theft the less theft because it is countenanced by usage, or accompanied by failure in understood duty."*

Soon after he was fifteen years of age, John Ridgway began to work. His father, we have seen, was a potter, and the son became this, too. The business suited his taste as well as his interest, and he gave himself to it thoroughly. Not as a master did he begin, but humbly as a servant. He had the business to learn, and he learnt it, entering into its various details, both of manufacture and commerce, throwing the energy of a

* *Modern Painters*, vol. v. p. 266.

strong will into every department with which he had to do, and finding not fatigue, but excitement and pleasure in almost every kind of labour. When he was short of twenty-three years old, he was deemed eligible for partnership in the business. He and his brother were admitted to this privilege at the same time, and on equal terms. Their partnership continued long after the father's death. In 1830 it was dissolved by mutual consent, at which time, and for a considerable period after, Cauldon Place became John Ridgway's alone.

The Pottery district has no town of any great size; nor is it, properly speaking, a cluster of small towns, but a continuous succession of such, strung, so to speak, on a zigzag line of road, extending— from one end to the other—a distance of about eight or ten miles. Each town is very much like the other, save in size or situation; and no one possesses much, apart from its "banks" or manufactories, to attract the notice of strangers. But when the elder Wedgwood commenced business, at the beginning of the latter half of the last century, there was scarcely any town at all. As early as the reign of Elizabeth the district was known for its earthenware productions of a common domestic kind; but not until very recent times did its stray, scattered houses and hamlets begin to assume the importance of towns. Even sixty years ago there were no lighted streets, and but few *streets* to light; no regular supply of water, or properly constituted markets, though a population large enough to require both; no hall for the administration of justice, and no local magistrate to administer it; no public rooms for popular assembly or for social festivity; no charitable institutions, or schools for the education of the young, save a few private ones; of churches and chapels but a very small number; and of conveniences for travel a supply so scanty, that there was only one stage-coach passing through from Liverpool to London, at the steady pace of five or six miles an hour.

From this may be gathered, if not precisely, yet some general idea of what the pottery manufacture itself was; for the development in one locality on any large scale of a particular branch of industry is sure to show itself in some corresponding degree in the rise of public institutions, and the growth of well-regulated towns. Whatever antiquity may be claimed for the manufacture of earthenware in the Staffordshire Potteries, it is to Mr. Wedgwood mainly that its present importance is to be attributed. His was one of those original and enterprising minds which results already attained can never satisfy: which see undreamt-of possibilities in the rudest performances and the simplest elements, as one may see the future beauty and kingly majesty of the forest oak in the sapling just planted or the acorn newly sown; and which, seizing with a strong hand the clue that is to conduct them through winding labyrinths of oft-repeated discouragement to the realization of their dreams, pursue this object with a zeal and patience unwearied by long seasons of hope deferred, until at length success, and more than success, becomes the reward of their exertions. Up to his time, the pottery trade can hardly be said to have existed in this country. The rich obtained their porcelain from China, the poor their earthenware from Holland. The art, so beautiful when genius takes it in hand, had yet to be created. Sedulously cultivated by some of the ancients, as also in modern times by the Germans and the French, it had to win its first triumphs amongst us. The single attempts that had been made to improve it had in a good degree ended in failure. The variety of design and richness of ornamentation which now distinguish our ceramic wares were scarcely then thought of, even in fancy; much less was it imagined that the time would ever come when the manufacture would so improve in quality, that £1,000 would be paid for a single service of turquoise and parian, and so increase in quantity, that the value of the exports from the

United Kingdom would amount in one year to about a million and a-half sterling.*

Wedgwood was throughout more anxious for distinction than for wealth, though in acquiring the former he acquired also the latter. He loved the art of pottery itself, and hence his wonderful success in it. Commencing business on his own account, or at first in partnership with another workman, without capital and with no preliminary training but that obtained at the potter's wheel, he at once struck out a line for himself, making, instead of the common ware of coarse material then known to the district, a variety of articles in imitation of agate, marble, tortoise-shell, and other like natural productions. From this step he advanced to another, and thence onward, with the courage and persistence of true genius—at least, with the resolution and patience of a noble ambition. He studied the chemistry of his day, courted the society of scientific men, employed artists of the greatest ability, as the celebrated Flaxman, to furnish him with new designs; thus pressing into the service of his art whatever science and skill could then supply. Encouragement came with every new achievement. His fame brought him not only increase of business, but additional facilities of improvement. Persons of taste opened to

* *Encyclopædia Britannica.* Article "Pottery and Porcelain."

him their costly fictile treasures. Vases, cameos, medallions, specimens of oriental china, &c., were freely lent to him; and all were ingeniously copied or employed for suggestion in the production of similar designs. Some of these were so expensive in the imitation, because involving so much care and delicacy in the workmanship, that he is said to have lost money by them; but he gained what is better, the gratification of complete success. This was the case in respect to that precious relic of ancient art, the Barberini vase, for which the Duchess of Portland had just given no less a sum than 1,800 guineas. Fifty copies of this were executed, when the mould was destroyed; but, notwithstanding they sold for fifty guineas each, they failed to pay the cost of making. It was enough, however, to have succeeded in this as in some other work. If more was wanted, it was obtained in a gradually widening reputation, and ultimately in the acquisition of fortune itself, though not by imitations of the antique so much as by branches of manufacture more serviceable for ordinary use. Of these latter there were several, but one became specially celebrated, and for this reason specially profitable. The Queen herself chose a service of it, gave permission to call it by her name, and honoured the maker of it by appointing him "Potter to Her Majesty."

This distinction, prized by Mr. Wedgwood almost above every other, was subsequently enjoyed by Mr. Ridgway. He became to Queen Victoria what Mr. Wedgwood was to Queen Charlotte. Not, however, until after many years of toilsome, though meritorious labour. Nor even then because he had done for the pottery manufacture what Mr. Wedgwood had done: but still for services that were deemed not unworthy of the honour. He came into possession of much that individual experience had made common, and added to it enterprise and taste of his own. Governed by no sordid desire of wealth, he had regard no less to the character of his work than to the pecuniary profit of it. Like most manufacturers, he wished for a large business, but he wished quite as much for a *good* business; and with him the test of goodness was not alone the credit of those who bought, but also the quality of what was sold. He had a love of excellence for its own sake, and this was sufficiently strong to seek for gratification, if not apart from gain, yet ever in connexion with it. This indeed always distinguishes the true workman from the mere speculator, or the selfish money-maker. It gives to manufacture the dignity of art, and converts business into an organ of benevolence. It turns the workshop into a school, and the work that is

E

done into a daily process of self-improvement. By its means labour loses more than half its toil, because of the mind that is engaged upon it; while the customary reward of weekly labour in weekly wages is supplemented by the much more precious reward of developed intelligence and cultivated taste.

But Mr. Ridgway's mind was eminently practical, and hardly anything would satisfy his desire that did not serve some useful end. And by useful, I mean not the gratification of an æsthetical affection merely, though this when duly appraised is not to be reckoned among the minor utilities, but the communication of some positive advantage over and above the pleasurable feeling excited. His love of excellence, therefore, was ever combined with a desire for service. Others might advocate the theory that the sole end of some things is to be beautiful, but to him beauty was scarcely a sufficient end in anything. He must have use, according to the popular notion of it; yet this consistently with as much that is not popularly deemed useful as could be economically joined with it. Hence he had no temptation, whether by original designs or by elaborate imitations of the antique, to add to the number of those rare productions of artistic genius, which, whatever their perfection of workmanship, serve exclusively for ornament. His very instinct led him, apart from any calculations of profit and loss, to eschew the curious and the costly in a preference for that which would be more serviceable in the supply of ordinary wants; while yet his taste and liking for what is intrinsically good and graceful demanded that even the common should not be coarse, nor the cheap without chasteness, but that, in every case where the two could be well combined, utility should be the ground on which beauty should be displayed. Here was his peculiar excellence. This was the secret of his success, for succeed he did in advancing the interest of the pottery manufacture generally in the district where he lived, particularly in the quality of its porcelain; and if he did not succeed in making what in these days of millionaires would be called a large fortune, the reason is to be found in causes which furnish a claim to far higher consideration than could be accorded to any mere manufacturer, however princely his gains. His success was ungrudgingly acknowledged even in his own locality, where rivalry might be supposed to detract from his merit. The historian of Stoke-upon-Trent says, "His porcelain has obtained the greatest celebrity for its beauty of design and embellishment, and for its purity, transparency, and perfect approximation to Sèvres china." He was singled out, we have seen, for the honour of a royal appointment, and the value of this honour was all the greater as no one thought it unworthily bestowed. Other distinctions followed, which may possibly be referred to afterwards; but one is entitled to particular mention here. Mr. Ridgway did not confine his regards to his own establishment. He sought to improve others by improving the trade in general, and to do this by improving the people themselves—as in many ways, so particularly by means of art-education. On his retirement from business in 1858, this was not forgotten, but classed among his many other claims to the gratitude of those among whom he had lived so long and worked so nobly. A public testimonial was presented to him, in acknowledgment of his high character as a manufacturer, and of the eminent services he had rendered to the district. One part of this testimony was in money; not, certainly, that he needed it but, probably, as making what was done more acceptable to him, by gratifying his known disinterestedness in furnishing him with an opportunity of connecting his own honour with the public good. If this was the motive, the end was well secured. The money presented was immediately consecrated to the founding of a scholarship in connexion with a School of Design which he had done much to establish and to foster. So, what was meant as a recognition of services already past, was turned into an enduring means of services yet to come.

In the *Illustrated Catalogue of the Art Journal*, devoted to a criticism on some of the many contributions to the Great International Exhibition of 1851, it is said, together with other commendation freely bestowed, "The establishment of Mr. Ridgway is one of the largest, and among the *best conducted* of the many factories of Staffordshire." This is said with especial reference to the manufacture there carried on; but it is true on other and higher grounds. According to the meaning intended, the establishment might be well conducted though the master was unknown to the workpeople; but in a sense of deeper moment, it could be well conducted only as the two were bound together in cordial relationships and by mutual services.

This well conducting of commercial establishments is one of the great wants of our times. The necessity has become imperative, and no large employer of labour can neglect the duty without perilling the good order of society, and accumulating to himself a fearful amount of personal responsibility. In our day trade has grown to enormous proportions, while the wealth accruing from it has sometimes threatened to outrival every other power. The steady increase of our home population has necessitated a large increase in our manufacturing productions. This result has been aided by the growth of our colonies, as also by the wants on a larger scale of other countries for those articles which we have the best facilities of making. The supply has hitherto overtaken the demand, and even urged it forward. Indeed, it must, since no limits can be assigned to human ingenuity, be practically inexhaustible. The problem has been, how to produce with the greatest economy and rapidity—a problem arising partly out of the demand itself, but still more, perhaps, out of that passion for riches so characteristic of our times, which has brought a multitude of competitors into the field. The solution is given in the cunning application of science to every species of industrial art; in that almost infinite division of labour which in most cases restricts a man's work to the doing of one thing, exacting even in this little more than a brief and oft-repeated mechanical process; especially in those wonderful inventions of human genius by which the powers of material nature are elicited into man's service in a thousand different ways, contracting space, abridging time, multiplying operations and results beyond all previous calculations of reason, or even dreams of fable. This solution has involved the creation of great manufacturing centres—the drafting into single establishments of individual workmen otherwise scattered, and the placing of them, in some common relation of dependence, under the authority of one or more masters. Such establishments are sometimes founded even where labour is incapable of minute division, where it is still what is called skilled labour—the production, that is, not of ingenious machinery, but of active brains and dexterous hands. In not a few instances, where venturous speculation tries its wing, or accumulated capital seeks for a profitable investment, these industrial hives are of such prodigious magnitude, that the number of men employed in them is equal to the population of one of our largest villages. What, then, must be the influence of those who stand at their head? And, with their influence, what their duty?

Very selfishly in many cases, and in a spirit much too narrow in most, has this latter question been answered. The answer given in effect is seen, not perhaps in the positive creation of another class, with wealth for its distinctive title—for this is the necessary growth of commerce itself—yet assuredly in such a separation between this class and the one lower down in the social scale, as generates the notion that their interests are conflicting and not identical; as often prevents their harmonious working for the common good, and sometimes shows itself in open resentment and violent outbreak. Generally, the only answer returned is restricted to the single item of wages, with no thought of any obligation beyond these; as if it must be admitted, and need not therefore be questioned, that the intention of Providence, in placing or allowing to be placed one man over hundreds and thousands of his fellow-men, and in such relation as to give him an influence over them most mighty for either good or evil, is fulfilled, with no further account to be discharged, in the mere payment of so much money for so much work.* Happily there are many exceptions to this, and these are becoming continually more numerous. While eminent philanthropists have in their own way done much to

* It ought, on the other side, to be observed, that the labouring classes often look with a most unjust, because unreasoning, hostility on those whose capital gives them employment. They watch, with a jealousy that leads to cruel misconstruction, the very acts which could hardly have anything but benevolence for their motive. I knew one case of a master, who in other respects had done much for the general welfare of his workpeople, taking great pains to supply, in connexion with his own establishment, the lack so often complained of in the housekeeping capability of those

relieve the hard oppression of what is nevertheless inevitable toil, not a few employers of labour, great and small, have exhibited in systematic and repeated efforts a most honourable concern for the well-being—personal, domestic, and social—of those whose industry is the immediate source of their wealth. Perhaps the sharp experience of the past has tended to this result. Both our literature and legislation have certainly had a share in it; so, let us believe, has the direct influence of Christianity, in giving a juster conception of personal responsibility, as in other relations of social life, so in that existing between masters and men. But much more of the same kind remains to be done, and much more must be done, especially by Christian merchants and manufacturers, if our commerce is to be redeemed from the charge of a selfishness which thinks only of gain, and the working and the wealthy classes are to be united by a bond more safe and more sacred than that of capital and labour. What is wanted is, that

females whose early life is spent in the warehouse or the mill. Among other means adopted, the least costly to him was the distribution of a book containing a number of recipes for cheap and substantial dishes for the table. So long as trade continued good, no objection to this was manifested; but when great scarcity and high-priced materials compelled an abridgment of labour and remuneration, this friendly act was interpreted as evidence of a design to prepare the people for living on reduced wages.

workmen shall be accounted something more than "hands;" that hands shall be seen in living connexion with hearts and homes; and that in every estimate of the hands, hearts and homes shall enter in the just proportion of their value.

These remarks are not intended as the introduction to an unqualified eulogy on Mr. Ridgway as a manufacturer, but they are intended to prepare the way for the statement, that few in this relation have obtained a character so unexceptionable as he. In the obituaries of him, published in the journals of the district immediately after his death, praise in this particular is accorded in no stinted measure. One quotation will serve for example. "As an employer," says the *Stafford Advertiser*, "Mr. Ridgway was a pattern master, for he remembered that he also had a Master in heaven. He had a well-selected, well-ordered, and superior set of workpeople, who repaid his solicitude for their welfare with devotion to his interests and affectionate regard towards himself." This, I believe, was written by one who had ample opportunities of knowing the truth, and yet who was free from those personal partialities which are of themselves a strong temptation to say more than is true. It is only, in fact, the common testimony put in print. The character here given of Mr. Ridgway's workpeople is so undeniable, that to be one of them was deemed of some special account; so that each had a sort of pride in saying that he worked at Cauldon Place. Their esteem of him rose to a positive affection, an affection that was directly personal, over and above, that is, the friendly feeling commonly generated by a good understanding between master and men in merely business transactions. Beautifully was this exemplified on the occasion of his ceasing to be their employer, in their uniting with the whole township to do him honour: yet, not by contributing to the general testimonial that was designed for him, but by presenting a testimonial of their own; and this, neither a valuable gift in money, nor a costly service of silver or of gold, but a Bible, large and superbly bound—as if anything only human was an insufficient or inappropriate expression of their regard; or rather, perhaps, that by this conclusive act they might attest in fitting symbol the conclusion to which their own experience had led them—that the teachings of the Word of God had been the principles by which his conduct towards them had ever been regulated.

Now, considering how little affection there ordinarily is between employer and employed— considering what positive enmities frequently spring up between them from the known difficulty of harmonizing their several interests, or of making that harmony apparent to both at the same time—this alleged "devotion" to Mr. Ridgway of his workpeople finding a last expression in an act so full of touching suggestion, is something to be specially accounted for, and can be accounted for only on the ground that he took, or endeavoured to take—however from human weakness he might sometimes fail—the Book, of which so magnificent a copy was presented to him for a memorial of their mutual connexion, as the directory of his conduct in all his dealings with them. This would certainly make him, as nothing else could, "a pattern master"; as this, besides its other instruction, fitting into every duty of life, would remind him with perpetual admonition, "that he also had a Master in heaven."

As this ground would afford a sufficient explanation, so, we may believe, the explanation itself is the true one. The Word of God was undoubtedly very familiar to him. There had scarcely been a time in his history when he had not known something of it. Its syllables were among the first that fell on his ear in his father's house. From childhood upward he had heard it read morning and evening in the family exercises, of which, he tells us, he "failed to call to mind a single omission." In early youth he read it for himself. Still later on he studied it, that he might expound it to others. It was thus to him as a continual presence, and must have been as a continual preacher. Its counsels would be in his memory as a voice ever sounding from above; its spirit would be in his heart, as a power constraining him, by many a secret impression, to follow their guidance.

Not carelessly, therefore, would he overlook, nor unwillingly adopt, the apostolic exhortation, "Masters, give unto your servants that which is just and equal." That in no instance he omitted to do this it would be unsafe to affirm, for human infirmity admits of no such perfection. But that he did this as a rule, and desired to do it always, is an inference as strong as directest proof from that "devotion to his interests and affectionate regard to himself" which his workpeople are known to have cherished; for no workpeople can have a kindly, much less an affectionate, feeling towards their employer, whose behaviour to them does not satisfy their sense of what is right. To do justly was certainly his aim. This feeling was at the bottom of his conduct as a master, though it might, from some reigning influence at the moment, be led astray in particular acts. It was strong enough to save him from that one-sided estimate of justice which is sure to be formed by the want of an equitable balance in the individual conscience, or by the discolorations of self, when that is the only medium chosen to look through. But once satisfied of the rectitude of a course, he was ready to stand by it, and, where compromise could not be admitted without wrong to others as well as himself, to brave obloquy for it.

In one or two instances of local disturbance, arising from trade disagreements, this necessity was forced upon him; and though really among the best and most esteemed of those on the same side of the quarrel, yet because he had the courage to place himself in the van of the defence, when others equally interested, or more so, were unable or unwilling to do this, he became, so long as the unreasoning excitement lasted, if not the least respected, the most abused of all: for popular passion is little accustomed to discriminate, and sometimes even selects as the objects of its special displeasure those most entitled to special regard, because that which so entitles them puts them in the foremost rank, and also becomes a power which popular passion has most reason to fear. Yet at these times of open discontent, and in presence of a tumultuous assembly, he could and did command a hearing when others would have failed. This was partly owing to the feeling of respect which after all lay deep and untroubled beneath the billows which the passing wind had fretted into anger; partly to that mysterious force of will which he could wield with almost irresistible effect over all who were fairly brought under its sway; and partly also to a peculiarly skilful address, with a genial humour for its momentary inspiration, which could readily hit the popular fancy by an ingenious improvement of some occurring circumstance, or disarm its resentment by a rejoinder which afforded no immediate opportunity of reply. It was on one of these occasions, that boldly presenting himself before a public meeting in the Hanley market-place, to which his friends had strongly advised him not to go, he was met on his rising to speak with a shower of abusive epithets, of which "Beelzebub!" was manifestly most in favour. "Beelzebub! Beelzebub!" rang through the mob as he essayed to open his mouth; but, with manner self-possessed, and a voice penetrating to the outer rim of the crowd, he quickly replied, thereby obtaining the hearing desired, "Ah! they called my Master Beelzebub, and no wonder that the humblest of His disciples should be so called."

It is plain, however, that no merely equitable relations existing between them—no positive commercial justice rendered by one and recognised by the other—would be a sufficient explanation of the attachment felt by Mr. Ridgway's workpeople personally to himself. This had a further ground in the practical interest he took in their well-being universally. He did not, as too many do, isolate himself from them by an indifference which allows of no approach, and looks for no opportunities of kindly service beyond the walls of the manufactory. He knew them in the street, and had for them a friendly greeting there. He advocated their social rights, or what he believed to be such, in advocating the social rights of their class; and this not languidly or under the stimulus of urgent occasions, but conscientiously, and with earnest and persistent effort. He took account of their homes, the education of their children, their times of sickness and of special need; and in relation to each made himself their counsellor and friend. While he knew how to be stern, he knew quite as well how to be tender. His kindness of heart could always be reckoned upon, albeit not as a weakness, but as a principle. He would excuse no disregard of his claims as a master—would rigorously exact what was due, where duty could be discharged, having in this respect regard no less to the good of his servants than of himself; but he was ever ready to help, where help was deserved and needed, and even where not deserved, the help, because needed, was often secretly given. It is surely unnecessary to say, in order to avoid the charge of undue commendation, that single individuals sometimes accused him of wrong; that occasionally some one would be found to speak of him with great harshness; that in particular acts he was possibly blameworthy, being led astray at the time by ignorance, or prejudice, or a spirit too hot and hasty. All this may be conceded, and more than this; yet, after every reasonable admission of this kind, it still remains true that those who served under him loved him as few employers are loved; and equally true, that by a courteous bearing, which never descended to rudeness, even in the ordinary transactions of business —by a generous sympathy, which was far more liable to be imposed upon than exhausted—by a placableness of temper which quickly brought back the receding tide of good-will, when some real or supposed offence had been given, especially by a religious concern, which thought of more than material interests, and expressed itself both publicly and privately in many honourable ways of deed and gift—he deserved to be loved as only few employers do.

This last reason is worthy of particular note. It forms Mr. Ridgway's highest distinction in the relation in which we now view him. He was a

F

large and successful manufacturer; but he was also something better, he was a Christian manufacturer. I mean that he was Christian, not in any nominal or conventional sense, nor because he had a general sentiment of religion which constrained him to a certain observance and support of Christian institutions, but by inward experience and open profession. He knew what conversion was, what a passing from death unto life is, what a precious provision for the daily supply of man's deepest needs is that grace of God which bringeth salvation; and he was not ashamed to say so. Ashamed! he accounted nothing so honourable. What he enjoyed, he was fain, in some way, to publish. He knew that not to profess was not to know, as not to shine is really to have no light. Decisively on the Lord's side, he would have deemed it treachery to conceal it. It could never have occurred to him to conceal it. Had he, under any temptation, so much as attempted this, he must soon, with the prophet, have been compelled to say, "His word was in mine heart as a burning fire shut up in my bones, and I was weary with forbearing, and I could not be silent." Not that there was ostentation in his profession; but there was reality, consistency, uniformity. He did not reserve it for the Sabbath, or the sanctuary, or for duties strictly religious. He carried it into business, into politics, into every social relation. It was known publicly by public acts, or rather by a public life; for he lived in the eye of the whole district, and any one that knew him at all, or in any capacity, knew him chiefly as a devout and active member of a Christian society. Always occupying the foreground in whatever scene was locally enacted, it was always as a professedly godly man that he was beheld there.

This involved him in peculiar responsibilities. It gave to the public, and to his own men in particular, a severer test by which to judge of him than the one commonly applied. It made his position as a master more critical, by provoking a harsher construction of his conduct, and a more suspicious scrutiny of his motives. For even the most irreligious are ready to exact from a Christian employer the utmost which a liberal interpretation of Christian duty on the side of their own interest demands, and to visit with a heavier condemnation the failure to render this, than would be thought of as due to a like failure in any one else; though, in fact, the obligation, so far as *their* claim is concerned, is not greater in the one case than in the other. Mr. Ridgway knew all this. He accepted the pledges which his active profession of godliness gave to those under him of a more than ordinary concern for their welfare. What is more, he redeemed them. The proof of this is found in what his workpeople thought of him, and continued to think to the last; in that "affectionate regard" already spoken of, which manifested itself not only in their fidelity as servants, but in an identification with his interests so complete as to give them a personal share in all that publicly concerned him. Not a few of them were members of the same church as he, though the only influence used on his part to make them so was the influence of that true-hearted piety which ever desires the salvation of those who are near to us. Doubtless he had, as we shall see, a decided preference for one particular religious community; but this was held subordinately to that deeper feeling which rejoices far more in the conversion of sinners than in accessions to any single society, and consistently with that regard for the authority of individual conscience which neither commits nor tolerates any trespass on its rights. A still larger number worshipped in the same sanctuary, or in another one which his liberality had built for their use, and for the use of their neighbours. He was frequently before them in the public discharge of religious duties. The master was often the minister, and no lay preacher was heard with more pleasure or profit. In his daily intercourse with them, religion, though not obtruded, was not forgotten. He would speak of it as a familiar interest with those who knew what it was, as a solemn necessity with those who knew nothing of it, and yet without soiling its sacredness by a want of propriety, either in the season or the manner. He would mingle with them at the close of the day, or on the Sabbath-day, in the most intimate exercises of Christian fellowship, such as Methodism specially delights in—would join with them in the freest conversation on divine things, or in mutual prayer for the blessing of God on themselves or on others; no feeling meanwhile coming between them to mar the profit of their service, arising from recollections connecting the place of business with the place for prayer.

So again in the vestry, when the business of the church called them together, he would meet with them, or with those holding a similar office to his, on precisely equal terms, ready to help with counsel or co-operate in labour; each of them exercising as true a liberty of speech and action as though the only relation which bound them to him was the one which bound them all to Christ. Now and then this liberty would be used without much discretion—not always, though occasionally it might be, because some excuse was given for the excess in a passing warmth of manner on his part; but rather from that pride of weakness which fears the suspicion of a too ready compliance with the suggestions of another, and which is tempted into opposition for the mere sake of realizing its own so-called "independence." But this was readily forgiven, as at other times he desired forgiveness himself; more, it was improved into a positive opportunity of doing good: for he knew how—as well from a sense of Christian duty, as because resentment could no more linger in his breast than hoar frost could linger beneath a vernal sun—both to "gain his brother," and to make him twice as much a friend as before. Thus, on one occasion, advocating with his customary earnestness a certain view to which he attached some importance, he was met by one present in a spirit of resolute resistance. Little reason appeared for the opposition, and hardly any sympathy was excited in support of it; still it was continued until it became violent, and even personal. The view was easily carried, for the judgment of the meeting was with it; but defeat did nothing to soothe the irritation of the angry dissentient. On the following day Mr. Ridgway sent for him to his office, intending only a friendly interview, but to his message the ill-natured reply was returned,

"Mr. Ridgway knows where I work; if he wants me, let him come to me." "Very well," was the only answer then given—it being plain, however, that a visit to him at that moment, especially in presence of one or more of his fellow-workmen, was not the meetest thing for the occasion. But the visit was only postponed to be paid under circumstances more favourable. In the evening the master was on his way to the home of the servant, which was at a considerable distance from his own home. His approach was observed by one of the family, and created some fluttering of heart. The latch of the door was raised, and Mr. Ridgway entering, with that bland and radiant countenance so familiar to those who knew him, pressed up to the offended and offending brother, who sat in the corner like a self-convicted culprit, and in a moment won him back to his better nature by the friendly greeting, "Well, ——, as you would not come to see me, I have come to see you."

It is needless to add more in this connexion. Further enlargement would only be further illustration of the same thing. He who in relation to those serving under him could live and act as we have described, and this for a space of nearly fifty years—not losing, but rather gaining all the time upon their esteem—must be, if not a "pattern master," yet one entitled to take his place with the very best. His character, considered simply as an exhibition of Christian principle, has something of positive greatness in it, uniting to the ordinary attributes of personal piety a consistency and magnanimity which belong to its highest distinctions. His position, considered relatively to others, is one to excite our envy,—at least, the envy of those who occupy a like commercial rank, as being a position of greatest honour and usefulness. Unhappily, it is not for this reason that the position, or any similar one, is generally coveted. In the pursuit of business, honour is less thought of than wealth, and usefulness less than honour. Trade is followed directly for its worldly advantages, while worldly advantages are desired, not as means to ends better and nobler, but as ends complete in themselves. Out of this spirit nothing great or good can ever come. It possesses no power to bless the individual, and none therefore to make him, except as he does not design it, a blessing to others. There is no feeling of responsibility in it, no impulse of benevolence. It is wanting in the only object which can dignify enterprise, and in the only motive which can sanctify labour. It is a mistake every way, both as policy and as duty: as policy, because it always fails in the satisfaction it looks for; as duty, because it utterly disregards the obligations of religion. When fairly estimated—estimated not in the light of a conventional respectability, but by reason and faith—it is not surely much for a man to be a merchant, though a rich one, or a manufacturer, though a large one. At the most, he obtains thereby somewhat more of this world's good than he can consume upon himself; and, at the best, gives employment to a number of individuals for whom he has not a moment's care beyond their worth to him as instruments for the increase of his gains. But to be this, and yet a Christian throughout—to carry into the sphere it opens a distinct recognition of claims which no attention to material interests can satisfy—to use the position it gives as a ministry of religious service to others, turning its advantages of wealth and influence to some positive account in the furtherance of purely spiritual objects—this, besides the present blessedness of becoming rich toward God, and the future recompense of treasure laid up in heaven, is to add to the character of merchant or manufacturer the unspeakably higher character of a public benefactor and a Christian philanthropist.

CHAPTER IV.

The Elder of the Church.

CHAPTER IV.

THE ELDER OF THE CHURCH.

In Mr. Wesley's *Journal* are the following entries, with some others relating to the places mentioned, which, though but remotely connected with our narrative, are not without interest to it.

"1760, March 8th.—Went from Wolverhampton to Burslem, a scattered town on the top of a hill, inhabited almost entirely by potters, a multitude of whom assembled at five in the evening. Deep attention sat on every face, though as yet accompanied with deep ignorance. But, if the heart be toward God, He will in due time enlighten the understanding."

"Sunday, 9th.—I preached at eight, to near double the number: some quite innocent of thought; five or six laughing and talking till I had near done, and one of them threw a clod of earth which struck me on the side of the head; but it neither disturbed me nor the congregation."

"1781, March 28th.—I returned to Burslem. How is the whole face of this country changed in about twenty years! Since the potteries were introduced, inhabitants have continually flowed in from every side. Hence the wilderness has literally become a fruitful field. Houses, villages, towns have sprung up. And the country is not more improved than the people. The Word of God has had free course among them. Sinners are daily awakened and converted to God; and believers grow in the knowledge of Christ. In the evening the house was filled with people, and with the presence of God. This constrained me to extend the service a good deal longer than I am accustomed to do."

The change in the face of the country, noticed by Mr. Wesley, was largely the fruit of Mr. Wedgwood's labours, of his great manufacturing success, and also of his public spirit; though not of his alone, for he found many imitators and helpers. Burslem was his home, his place of business; and it soon grew, by means of his industrial achievements, into a town of considerable local importance. For this reason Mr. Wesley often visited it—perhaps also for a further reason; for, in another part of his *Journal*, he says, with manifest pleasure, "We had there our first society in the country, and it is still the largest and the most in earnest." Hanley, now the most attractive of all the Pottery towns, was then but a village, and, though picturesquely situated, scattered and mean-looking. It was, with reference to Methodism, a dependency on Burslem; while even Burslem, up to the date of the above extract, held a subordinate relation to Macclesfield. The great apostle of Methodism could hardly, then, be expected to see much of Hanley, his visits being of most value where most people could be addressed. Still he was there on several occasions, and one visit is thus recorded: "1784, March 30th.—I preached in the new preaching-house at Hanley Green; but this was far too small to hold the congregation. Indeed, this country is all on fire, and the flame is still spreading from village to village."

Mr. Ridgway's father had much to do with kindling this flame in Hanley. The fire was there before he came to the place, or rather before he returned to it from Leeds, where for an interval of some years he had lived. But he brought to it some contributions of his own, and did not a little to keep it alive. His was one of those energetic and generous, though not always thoughtful and sympathizing spirits, which know nothing of weariness and languor; and which, as if by a plethora of individual life, communicate life to all about them. Besides, he was then glowing with the new ardours of a first love, and, with such a nature, was not likely to imprison the flame in his own breast. When he came to Hanley, " there was preaching only once a fortnight," and but one small class of members. He had not been settled there more than a few months, when, though only a young single man, he had gathered out of the world " a goodly tribe of twenty-five"; in which number, having steadfastly commenced his evangelizing work at home, were included his brother and his brother's wife, with whom he lived. What kind of place this little band had before made use of for their " preaching only once a fortnight," I know not; I suspect it was only a private house. But, " in the following spring," says Mr. Ridgway (he came to the Potteries the November preceding, 1781), " we provided a commodious room, and fitted it up during the succeeding year." This would be commodious only by comparison; in itself it was doubtless humble enough. But even this soon became inconveniently small: " So," adds the good man, a little farther on, " with great exertion we raised a temple for God, into which we entered with joy, and still prospered." This " temple" was the "new preaching-house" in which, on that 30th of March, 1784, the venerable Wesley—then venerable in the double sense of sanctity and of years—held forth the Word of life, and in which he saw the signs of that fire with which, as he testifies, the country was all a-glow. A *temple* it was to one; something much less than this to the other; yet to each precisely what he calls it. "And still prospered." The reminiscence is manifestly a pleasurable one. There is almost exultation in it, certainly a pious satisfaction and fond recollection of the past, which not even the thought that the writer has long been separated from the church to which it refers can in anywise diminish or disturb. They prospered because they deserved to prosper, so far as desert in such a case can be affirmed of any merely human agency. The "one class" became many, and the "preaching only once a fortnight" became several preachings within the same period. The "little one" grew, and grew so rapidly that it promised in good time to multiply into the prophetic "thousand."

But growth brings with it strength, and generates a spirit of self-reliance. Strength is seldom unconscious, and is therefore seldom content to have itself unnoticed. It comes into the possession of certain notions of right, and by force of these becomes persistent, possibly even troublesome, in its claims. Sometimes it asks under the name of liberty for what tutors and governors are apt to interpret as a dangerous license. Always it looks for recognition, for concession of something hitherto withheld; and as manhood comes on, demands at least to be delivered from the restraints, the denials, the routine, the petty but prudential oversight that befit a period of inexperience and youth.

It was so in this instance. The prosperity continued for several years. It pleased God by the foolishness of preaching to save them that believed, and the number of these was considerable. It required some courage, the courage of a thorough work of grace in the heart, to unite, at such a time, in such a neighbourhood, with a sect so spoken against as the Methodists then were. But the courage was found, because the grace was felt. Men were willing to bear the obloquy of being accounted Methodists, if only they might enjoy the blessedness of becoming Christians. With increasing numbers, the Society acquired a completer organization, and a greater power of self-management. With increasing piety, it demanded a larger extension of Christian privilege, in the institution of certain ordinances which had not as yet been administered within its own pale. The right to these was the right also to some other things entering essentially into the constitution and discipline of a Christian church; and this right was accordingly asserted. Out of this trouble came, and sorrow, and final separation. Sad is the chapter in the history of Methodism in general, and of this society in particular, which commences at this date; though the sadness has reference rather to the passions and prejudices, the rivalries and ruptures that marked its course, than to the conclusions to which it ultimately led, or to the lessons which it now teaches. For, sad as it is, the struggle it records, like most similar struggles, is one out of which much good has come, and some good not intended, through the gracious overruling of Him who is Head over all things to the Church. Nor to one party alone has the good come, but even to that one which professed no desire for the advantages sought for, or which then thought it inexpedient to claim and use them; for to this, the parent body of Methodists, has descended from that season of trial a heritage of privilege which it would not at any cost now part with, and could not at a cost less than that of self-destruction. It is not, then, in any spirit of controversy that I extract a page or two from this chapter in the history of the past, nor mainly with a view to vindicate any of the facts therein contained, but rather because some of these facts have such intimate connexion with the subject of our narrative that they cannot wholly be passed over.

It is thus Mr. Ridgway the elder writes:—
"The Society at Hanley wished to have the Lord's Supper administered, and we twice petitioned Conference on the subject; but though our prayer was unanimous, it was refused. It so happened that the majority of our trustees lived in Burslem, and, being high Churchmen, they took upon themselves to fix our times of preaching on the Saturday evening at seven o'clock, and on the Sabbath at seven and nine in the morning. We found these very unseasonable hours, and thought we had the right to fix our own time of worship, consistently with the plan of the circuit; but this matter proved a source of great opposition and uneasiness. About this time also it was that petitions were sent to Conference from most of the circuits for a redress of grievances, on account of the general dissatisfaction which prevailed. Meetings for this purpose (for petitioning) were held in different parts of the kingdom, and, amongst the rest, at Hanley. Preachers, trustees, leaders, and stewards assembled together, to petition Conference to adopt such measures as should conciliate the people, and make

the interests of preachers and people one. The meeting was opened with singing and prayer; the leading subjects of complaint were brought forward and freely discussed, and a vote passed on each particular. The result was, that a petition should be sent to the Conference, and Mr. Smith was appointed the delegate for that purpose. The substance of the petition was as follows:—

That no preacher should have power to receive or expel members but by the sanction of the leaders or quarterly meeting.

That the people should choose their own class-leaders.

That no one should preach to our people without having been previously approved by the quarterly meeting.

That no local preacher should be suspended, or silenced, but by the same authority.

That no persons should be called out to travel but such as were approved by the people amongst whom they lived, and were recommended by the quarterly meeting.

That one preacher and one lay delegate (chosen by the people) from each circuit or district, should compose the Conference; each having equal power in the transaction of all business.

That the lay delegates should take charge of all

moneys to the Conference, and attend to their disbursement.

The meeting was dissolved by the plenary power of the preachers and trustees, and those who had agreed to the petition, comprising nearly all present, were declared no longer members of the Society. Appeals were made against this procedure to the properly constituted meetings of the circuit, but, on the ground that those who made them were not now members, these appeals were dismissed. The petition was, nevertheless, taken to the following Conference—the celebrated Conference of 1797, held in Leeds—but, with many like petitions, was so rejected as to exclude all hope of mutual reconciliation, and of one sole united Methodist Community. Hence sprang into existence the Methodist New Connexion.

Melancholy and painful is the account Mr. Ridgway gives of the treatment which he and those concerned in the same movement received from such as had authority to oppose their wishes, but the repetition of it here could serve no useful purpose. Indeed, it is no gracious thing at any time to revive almost forgotten animosities; least of all is it this, when no such difference of principle as that which originally gave rise to them is under immediate discussion. Suffice it then to say, that those who had been dismembered formed a Society to themselves, but in recognised fellowship with a number of similar Societies in different parts of the country. Having men of energy and piety at the head, some of whom were also growing into respectable commercial positions, they soon acquired firmness and strength; the more so as they had, though under the disadvantages occasioned by the want of the regular ministry, a considerable increase of religious privileges. Indeed, they took away with them, when cut off from their former friends, much of the fire which Mr. Wesley had before observed in their midst, and this, burning with an ardour only increased by the memory of recent trials, continued still to spread, though from another centre. Shut out from the sanctuary which had been their home, and which, "with great exertion," they had helped to rear, they had at first nothing larger or better than a coach-house in which to worship; but this, says the narrative from which we quote, they "fitted up very comfortably, and had many a happy time in it." Soon the coach-house became too strait, and another house, more commodious and more fit, must be had. Not, however, on another site, for this had been hallowed by much prayer, and by many conversions to God. So in due time, on the same spot, a new sanctuary—sanctuary in the fullest sense—was erected, which has since been the parent of many other sanctuaries, and of several enlargements and transformations of itself, crowned and completed by that latest and last—for who could desire a fairer or larger—the holy and beautiful house, which all have admired for its fine proportions and simple finish, and which thousands both on earth and in heaven have loved, as well for their brethren and companions' sakes, as for its ministry of the Word and its service of song.

John Ridgway was eleven years of age when the "Division" took place. He may be said to have been present at the birth of the Methodist New Connexion. He certainly received, and bore into after life, some impressions of the throes and anguish which preceded it. He was old enough to know that strife was going on, and inquisitive enough to ask its meaning. The fact that parents whom he loved with almost more than a child's tenderness were concerned in it, quickened his observation of what was said and done in his presence. And much *was* said; much which he delighted afterwards to recall, and much more, doubtless, which grew dim in the distance of years.

His father's house had been the home of the preachers in former and peaceful times. They had often sat at his table, and often blessed him and his with religious conversation and prayer. The habit was still continued. It was the same home, and there the same hospitality was shown; but other preachers, or preachers serving another Community, though in the fellowship of the same Gospel, were now the welcome guests. These were present frequently, with other friends like-minded. Common misfortunes bound them in a more than common intimacy. Common views and sympathies gave them common interests and pursuits. There was much intercourse between them; the same topic of conversation, we may well believe, nearly always turning up, drawing the thought towards it, at least while the subject was fresh, by an almost irresistible attraction. Indignation, it may be, was sometimes expressed; perhaps an undue, yet not wholly unpardonable severity of feeling was now and then indulged in, as the memory of wrongs lately endured was freshened by some new recital of the past. Possibly this became in single instances even personal, as individuals were thought of whose weakness had suffered them to be seduced from a course which their judgments had deliberately commended. We know that there were many such, and in like circumstances would be many more. Sorrow there was at separation from friends hitherto beloved, and something, neither sorrow nor anger, but a feeling akin to both, at being compelled to commence a career of Christian activity as from a new starting point, though with precisely the same ultimate goal in view. There was doubtless much anxiety, though relieved and even brightened with much hope, as the future was looked into. But there were no misgivings and no regrets, no surrender of the ground taken, and no fear lest the ground should prove unsafe: for enlightened conviction, generating a steady resolve, had been at the root of the whole movement, and both conviction and resolve remained there still. So they strengthened one another's hands; looked difficulties fairly out of countenance; nourished in their hearts by mutual confidences and free discussion the sentiment of religious liberty, as they understood it; and parted and met, and met and parted to find their work of establishing a new Methodist Community, on some recognised basis of equal rights and common privileges, not wholly in vain in the Lord.

At these homely conferences John Ridgway was often present. Perhaps he sometimes stole in unawares, and remained unobserved. At other times he was seen gazing up into the speaker's face with attentive wonder and sympathy, as some tale of hardship from superintendent preacher or trustees was being told; or sidling between the knees of Kilham, of Thom, of Grundell, or of that good Mr. Smith, his father's partner in business, who, a little before his death, desired to be taken to the new sanctuary which he had greatly helped to build, that he might at least be present in it once more ere he entered the better sanctuary above, and who, on being borne to the pulpit (for he was a local preacher), first selected his own place of burial, and then, with the fervour of a Christian man standing consciously on the threshold of eternity, prayed that God would bless the word to be preached in that His house, as also the labours of His servants generally, in the conversion of thousands of souls. Tell a child a story of wrong and suffering, and you are sure of his indignation against the one that wrongs, and of his sympathy with the one that suffers. Let those he venerates or loves be the sufferers, and you make him in spirit a hero at once. Such a hero John Ridgway became as he listened to the recitals and conversations of these now sainted men, though even then with that peace-loving disposition which would rather right the wrong than avenge it. Many a time has he been heard to say, in recalling their sayings, and tracing back his own matured convictions of church polity to the impressions which their words produced on his mind, "When I stood between the knees of those honoured servants of God, and heard them speak of the trials and struggles which they and others had passed through in the maintenance of what they believed to be scriptural right and freedom, my little bosom beat and burned, and I resolved, if such resolution was possible to one so young, that in years to come, should I be spared, I would make their cause my own."

That he kept his word we know, though certainly not as a promise which was afterwards remembered, and must be held sacred—for in this sense the word was probably soon forgotten—but as a sentiment which then quickened within him for the first time, and subsequently grew, under circumstances favourable to its development, into the mastery of a regulative principle. It is otherwise in most cases, and for this reason perhaps the more commendable in him. The free spirit of childhood, the generous sympathy of youth, mostly harden into a fixed conservatism in age. To some extent this is unavoidable and natural. Experience leads to it, and demands it; and in thus demanding, justifies it. Only in too many instances the conservatism is deliberately chosen, and chosen from a too exclusive regard to personal interests, or the interests of a class. It then becomes inconsiderate and unjust, sometimes stolidly averse to all change whatever, and even selfishly despotic.

John Ridgway drank in Christian instruction and Christian liberty together. Two sets of lessons were given him at the same school, and mainly by the same teachers, each one it may be strengthening the impressions of the other, while much of both, as home teaching generally is, was given and received silently and unconsciously. By the one, God blessing the lessons to his conversion, he became in youth a member of the Methodist New Connexion; by the other, childish sympathy ripening into abiding conviction, he became in manhood an able advocate of its principles, and a munificent supporter of its institutions. To no other single individual, assuredly to no other single layman, does the Connexion owe so much. This, I think, may be said, after every deduction which an equitable, or even a rigorous criticism, would or could make from his services. Abridge them as you may, take as much from their value as you fairly can, and still the sum which remains to his account is, in any form of reckoning permitted to us, a result which one might well be content to live for.

The history of the Connexion would be very

much the history of his life. Or if this is too much to say, it is hardly questionable that after the first few years of its troubled and struggling existence, his life would be a convenient thread on which to string the main events of the half century following that marked its course. He had an early manhood, and his manhood continued, with a gathering strength and wisdom, to a mature age. His mind was eminently political and administrative, though, like most such minds, prone to over legislation and an excess of management. Many things are best taken care of when allowed to take care of themselves. Interference is impediment, and protection injury. Still, such a mind as his was specially called for when Providence gave him to the Connexion. There had hardly been time for a constitution to grow, or at least to take a definite working shape; for constitutions must grow, otherwise, whatever their speculative value, they have little practical utility. "They will not march," says Thomas Carlyle, speaking with grim merriment of the constitutions which emerged one after another out of the flood and chaos of the French Revolution. Or if there had been time by the measurement of years, there had been the want of other conditions equally necessary to full and final determinations. A few general principles had been agreed upon at first as the basis of fellowship and mutual action, and these had been steadily adhered to. No reason for departure from them had arisen; none was likely to arise. They formed, indeed, a solid foundation and framework, within which all that a personal liberty could desire, consistently with a Connexional organization, might be embraced. They have hence now (and this is the best commendation of the wisdom that framed them) precisely the same authority which they had then. But much was unsettled—uncertain—in a state of solution, awaiting the verdict of experience, or the appearing of some one who could read and construe into a fixed formula the verdict which experience had already pronounced. Hitherto strife, in sheer self-defence, had distracted the ablest intellects. Defection and repudiation, on the part of those who had professed friendship and responsibility, had distressed the most hopeful and generous hearts. "Labours more abundant"— labours that would now be deemed all but impossible—rendered necessary by the vast circumference of single circuits, and the number of preaching places included therein, as also by the desire to build up from dead stones everywhere lying about living societies that should be worthy to be called a Connexion, and a New Connexion —these consumed so much time, and demanded so much attention, that little of either was left, save for that small class of spirits which have never too much to do, and never tire of doing anything, for the less profitable, and to most minds less congenial task, of balancing questions of policy and forming codes of discipline.

These and other impediments to final conclusions on many points, which now seem to us simple and natural enough, still it is true existed, and were likely to exist for some time to come; but then they existed with a diminishing force, or, if not, with a diminishing effect. Besides, much experience had been gained, and this experience was all the more valuable, as it had been gained by means of sharp trial and suffering. The history of the past few years had been an eventful history, bringing forth a considerable harvest of facts, from which, if the requisite sagacity were applied, might be distilled maxims and rules that would serve for prudent legislation, giving to the whole Body a completer organization, and to its several parts a greater consistency and unity of action. The sagacity was not wanting when the occasion for it arose. John Ridgway was only one of several who possessed it in a good degree, but he was one of the chief. The juncture was favourable to his peculiar aptitudes and powers, and so, entering into the labours of predecessors who had toiled hard and done nobly, and uniting with others whose names and deeds are dear to us as household treasure, he then commenced that career of steadfast devotion to the interests of the Connexion which gave him, as "a ruling elder," a position and influence which no one else has ever acquired in the same Community, and which no one else is ever likely to acquire again.

This office of Ruling Elder is the capital distinction of the Methodist New Connexion. The admission of one so-called—or of one with the functions which the name suggests—to a partnership of power with the Teaching Elder, so as to give to the lay and clerical elements an equivalence of authority in all deliberative assemblies and legislative acts, is the one point of difference between its polity and that of the Community from which it separated. Other points existed at the beginning, though nearly all of them ran up, directly or by implication, into this principal one. But time brought with it concessions which gradually lessened their number, especially the concession which gave to the people the right, or rather which acknowledged their right, to have administered by their own "pastors and teachers" the ordinances of Baptism and the Lord's Supper. It were to be wished that, by a similar concession, the main distinction between the two bodies were annihilated. Not that the two might become substantially and organically one—though, considering their perfect agreement in doctrine and religious ordinance, this is surely something to be desired; but that at least every avoidable occasion of future controversy, and of the animosity springing therefrom, might be anticipated and prevented; that the traditions of the past, arising from contentions on this remaining element of difference, might, by a swifter process, wear themselves out in a more cordial intercourse and a freer interchange of Christian offices; that, most of all, the prayer of their common Saviour might be answered, as hitherto it has not been answered, in that greater impression upon the world which their joint activity and recognised oneness in Him could scarcely fail to produce. A special reason, and not the least important, for such concession is, that future rents and divisions in the same Body may be avoided—divisions which, for a time at least, weaken in many ways the Body itself, add to the already distracting number of Protestant communities in this country, and, what is worse, to the number of communities bearing the same general name, turn into heated polemics or partisans multitudes who should have no other concern than their own personal salvation, and produce at once the double evil of putting a stumbling-block in the way of the weak, and a weapon into the hands of the wicked.

Such divisions are sure to recur under a system which fosters the popular element as Methodism does, training it to every sphere of religious activity up to the very highest, yet denying it all share in those legislative acts for which in this very training a certain preparation is given, and by which, whatever repugnance may be felt to them, it must itself be bound. Again and again will they transpire, as questions arise to bring ministers and people, or a portion of them, into opposition to each other; for such questions must arise, so long as their mutual interests are not mutually considered, or as some individual ministers, with a following outside, are brought into visible collision with other ministers of higher standing and authority than themselves: for these are certain to obtain the sympathy of their friends, and to find enforcement of their cause in a companionship which must ultimately lead to separation. The only adequate safeguard against the evil appears to be, if the Presbyterian association of churches must be preserved, in a Presbyterian distribution of legislative and administrative power; or, in other words, in the admission of elders "that rule well," in some fair proportion of numbers, to an equal standing in all Church assemblies with elders "that labour in the word and doctrine."*

Such an elder, I have said, John Ridgway was. He was almost a personal embodiment of the very principle and spirit of the office. He was once called, outside his own Community, "the prince of delegates"; and if delegate be understood as equivalent to representative, he was not within

---

* These remarks, of course, would be of little worth against any clear showing from Scripture, that to the ministry belongs, inherently or by Divine bestowment, the right to govern the Church solely by its own authority—without, that is, the participation in legislative functions of those who are governed; though *could* this be shown, it would be hard to reconcile the teachings of Scripture with the demands of reason. Such showing, however, is impossible, and has often been proved to be so; while no one would surely pretend to the right itself but those to whom a priestly despotism is necessary for the support of a degenerate faith. The Church as a whole is one, and any particular church presents the same unity. It is not ministers or people, but ministers *and* people, fitly joined and compacted together. It should therefore be so governed as to preserve and exemplify this oneness; so governed as to be *self* governed. But it is self-governed only as the whole governs, either by an equal distribution of power among all the individual members, or by some system of representation which sums up the general will and articulates the universal voice.

the circle of Methodism without some claim to the appellation. But this was in the maturity of his powers, and when his usefulness had attained its meridian. He had not reached manhood when he began to interest himself in Church affairs. His exertions were, of course, at first local, and strictly religious, having for their immediate object his own and others' edification in the knowledge of Christ. They soon became Connexional, and so, in a more general sense, ecclesiastical. He was early in Conference, representing the circuit to which he belonged; and, before this, was taken into the counsels of his father, and two or three other friends who had represented the circuit from the beginning. Of that assembly he continued a member, with the exception of a single year now and then, up to the time of his death: not always as a representative chosen by his circuit, but still as a representative filling some office to which the previous Conference had elected him. He had delight in office, the delight of one who feels at home in it. Without seeking, he fell naturally into it, as the place for which he was designed. Its cares did not distract him, nor its business perplex. They were rather a pleasurable excitement, an excitement which he loved so well, that he was seldom unwilling to have the whole of it to himself. He had immense industry and application, a rapid perception of the whole merits of a case, a brain teeming with expedients, and a hand never weary of giving to them the form of specific resolution. He was in a high degree methodical, with a quality of mind that I know not how better to describe than as anticipative. His thoughts quickly took shape, and his concerns, however multifarious, soon fell into order. Few questions came before him which he had not foreseen, and for which he had not, often while other men slept, made some preparation. I have now memorandum books beside me containing the prospective business of many Conferences; of some Conferences the entire order of business, of others the matters of greatest exigency or interest, with suggestions and sketches of resolutions for their consideration and disposal. He was seldom seen, whether in committee or open Conference, without a bundle of papers, folded lengthwise, and neatly tied with red tape—filled from top to bottom in his broad, decisive, but somewhat sprawling hand—with preamble and recommendations intended to meet and cover the whole question which most were just beginning to think of for the first time. Now and then, especially at a later period, he found his plans crossed, and some of his work vain; but, nothing discouraged, he would address himself to the task again, deftly incorporating other work into his own, or seeking by new expedients to accomplish the same end, never for a moment relinquishing his object so long as it was tenable by almost any means whatever.

To some he appeared occasionally inconsistent in his change of plan, or unreasonably obstinate in the pursuit of his end; and doubtless was so to a certain extent: but probably this judgment would in many cases have been modified by a deeper acquaintance with his character. One that knew him well, who saw him daily and familiarly, as hardly any one else could see him, and who wants not the power to tell what he sees, thus speaks of him: "He had strength of conviction, for he held tenaciously to his principles. And these principles were not mere prejudices, although in some cases, as may be supposed, they might be pretty much so. Especially he had strength of will, and carried out his designs with indomitable energy and perseverance. . . . From the constitution of his moral nature, he was in the habit of looking at the end rather than the means, and where to superficial observers he appeared changeable or vacillating, he was simply so impressed with the importance of the end proposed to himself, which he kept steadily in view, that he was willing to change his plans again and again, provided he could see that the change promoted the object, and brought him nearer to the end of his journey. Whether the change was to conciliate friends, to remove obstacles, or in any way to facilitate the accomplishment of his wishes, the apparent vacillation was really the result of the steadfastness and perseverance which formed one of his most decided characteristics." This is said, it is right to observe, in connexion with a statement to the effect that his perception was so intuitive, that "he was seldom mistaken in his objects." The remarks are made with no particular reference to Church matters, but they apply in part to these as well as to the multitude of other affairs which crowded upon his attention daily.

With an aptitude for business, a love of it, an easy command of its details, a fertility of resources ever equal to its emergencies, he had great power in debate. He was a ready and skilful speaker. His presence was commanding, his voice was rich and sonorous, his features were large and radiant—save his eye, which was often gathered and contracted, as if for the advantage of a keener penetration, though relieved by the twinkle of good-humour that mostly played in its corners. He seldom hesitated. His words came freely, because his thoughts came naturally, bounding from his lips at once. He was often extremely adroit and neat in his turns of expression, especially if a compliment was to be paid, or an opponent to be won. He was cunning at fence, could parry a thrust or give one with considerable dexterity, expose the weak points of an adversary's case by a damaging criticism, and present the strong points of his own in a breadth of outline or dash of colour that would conceal for the moment whatever defects it might have. He was not by any means faultless in his language, not always unexceptionable in his taste, though remarkably epigrammatic and antithetical in his style. Effect was his object, to impress his convictions and policies upon others. He lost all consciousness of himself as a speaker, and thought only of what he said and of what he meant. "This man," said Mirabeau, of one who was to conduct a terrible episode in French history, "will do somewhat; he believes every word he says." This fulness of faith was observable in Mr. Ridgway. Himself thoroughly convinced, he began to speak intending to convince others, and to carry his convictions with all. It was hence he seldom failed. If the question was his own, he had by rapid, sometimes a too hasty preparation, its principal features firmly in his thought. If it was another's, he surveyed it, as the exposition or discussion proceeded, with quick and discriminating observation, seldom lifting his head from the paper on which he was writing to look the speaker right in the face. When he stood up to speak, you were obliged to listen. You saw, you felt that he was a power. He commenced slowly, though not falteringly; with reserve and self-control, even when feeling was preparing to boil over in some passionate conclusion. By a stroke of wit he disarmed an opponent, by a flash of humour put him in good temper, by a deferential courtesy gratified his self-love. Or, if in the character of an advocate, he began with grave and deliberate seriousness, choosing his expressions with calm and measured wisdom, deploying his facts and arguments with a tact and ingenuity that would at least insure for them an effective display. But, whether as advocate or adversary, he soon quickened his pace, grew warm, fluent, rapid, almost impetuous. If opposition had stirred him, impetuous he did become; his feeling kindled to excitement, and his manner to vehemence; his thoughts coursed each other like rain along a mountain side, and his words flew thick and fast like a shower of arrows from Ulyssean bows; his whole being spoke, feature and limb bearing the visible impress of the surging spirit within; and his speech from beginning to end was as the gathering force and volume of a wave, which, at first curling into a gentle ripple, comes careering on, till it finally breaks in thunder on the shore.

This kindling feeling, it may well be supposed, sometimes led Mr. Ridgway into error. The velocity acquired was such as to master him for the moment, and carry him beyond the line which his judgment would have selected for his farthest limit. He thereby wounded an opponent, or grieved a friend, without at the same time much furthering the object which himself had in view. But he hurt more than opponent or friend. His excitement came back with swift recoil upon himself. With great boldness he had great tenderness, and this tenderness exposed him to a painful self-chastisement. Nor was he reluctant to confess his error, but eager to make the first approach to a complete reconciliation with the person he had offended. I have before me a note written to a young member of Conference, exemplary of this. In a discussion on the revision of the Rules of the Connexion, in 1854, it was proposed by this juvenile member to restrict the right of appeal of those who for any reason had been cut off from Church fellowship to meetings or courts outside the jurisdiction of Conference. Hitherto the law had carried the right up to this last court, the highest of all. Mr. Ridgway and others desired to perpetuate this right. The discussion grew warm, and was long continued, but terminated in favour of the resolution; which resolution, however, was at a subsequent session reversed, on grounds which need not be stated here. In this question Mr. Ridgway took a great interest, throwing into the debate his whole strength of intellect and feeling. He was not personal, perhaps, yet he was severe,—harsh even, disposed almost to resent as an injury the loss of a victory which he had counted on as sure. But his words were thorns in his own breast. He could draw them out only in one way. He must leave early on Monday, for a Chancery suit called him to London. The following day was Sunday. So at five o'clock in the morning he was at his desk penning the following note:—

"Woodside, June 13th, 1854.

"MY DEAR SIR,—Conscience commands me, before I leave Halifax, to say that I fear I have been hasty in my bearing to you on the 'Appeal' question, and that as such I ought to acknowledge it, and ask your friendly absolution. I might offer many excuses for myself, but I prefer leaving it to your consideration to make them for me.

My zeal has been greater than my discretion. If I was right, I might have been more courteous; if I was all anxiety, I ought to have been more patient and forbearing. Well, be assured I have only the kindliest feeling to you; and, while tears drop from my overflowing eyes as I write this, let at least one drop from yours, and wash the incident away. I am thankful for the end; I deeply regret so much of the means. It will give you another instance of the imperfection of our naughty nature, and teach me that the means must be as amiable as the end is excellent. Adieu, my dear friend! Every blessing attend you and all yours. Faithfully yours,

"John Ridgway."

Though thus ardent in temperament, and, notwithstanding his natural courtesy, great urbanity, and prevailing good sense, prone now and then to be imperious and severe,—if, in the relation in which we now view him, Mr. Ridgway had one quality more striking than another, it was a spirit of compromise and accommodation, carried sometimes, where no leading interest could be sacrificed, almost to the verge of seeming weakness. He was a great reconciler, and appeared fond of the office. He was ever ready to mediate between judgments that were at variance or hearts that were estranged. He had a peculiar aptitude for adjusting different views of the same question, by finding out coincidences in which the differences might be reconciled, or some ground common to them all on which, when brought to meet, they might start out together in the same direction. His principles were too fixed and too vital for him to become a trimmer; but this, in some single instance, he might seem to a careless looker-on. The fact is, his mind was so diplomatic, his temper so reconciling, his fertility in expedients so abundant, while his purpose to accomplish a certain end was so resolute, that he could not but be a consummate politician.

With such attributes of character, Mr. Ridgway was admirably adapted for any ordinary deliberative assembly, and fitted soon to obtain great influence in it. Loving the religious Community to which he belonged with an ardour almost rare, even where such love existed at all, he was likely in any sphere suited to his powers which it called him to occupy to render it much more than ordinary service. Entering its Conference at a time when there was peculiar scope for such ability as he possessed, and promised to possess in a still more eminent degree, and continuing to attend its sessions, with only a very few omissions, for at least the space of fifty years, he was sure to acquire a high consideration in its counsels, and to exercise a great authority in its general transactions. The service he actually rendered would be a tedious history, branching out into many details, and comprehending a multitude of things of like kind. The Rules of the Connexion are so much his monument, that it requires only a certain familiarity with his style of expression to trace his hand in almost innumerable places; though the attesting peculiarites have to some extent disappeared under the last revision, which he lived just long enough to see commenced. The *Minutes*, annually published, are a still larger monument, containing in the form of resolutions very much of his own workmanship, and representing in connexion therewith even more than the qualities we have ascribed to him. Of his labours generally, in the capacity now under review, and of their serviceableness to the Body as a whole, one example will avail for illustration.

He had early, while a very young man, been impressed with the want of a legal settlement of the Connexion. In a series of papers which appeared in the Magazine for 1815, and which were afterwards published in a little work under the title of *An Apology for the Methodists of the New Connexion*, he gives this want as one of several reasons of the comparatively slow growth of the Connexion. His words are :—" The want of a legal constitution, I apprehend, has been a vital obstacle to its extensive spread. Destitute of this, its stability has been precarious, and even its integrity endangered. Not that I would hazard an opinion that this desideratum should have been agitated earlier. No: the best plans improve by experience; and until that test had demonstrated the sterling excellency of the system, it had been premature to seek for legal sanction. If, however, the Connexion has made its way without this pledge, confident I am that when the system is guaranteed and perpetuated by the laws of the land, it will take root and win its way." And in a note to this, which is worthy of being transcribed for the general principle it contains, he says:—" I am far from agreeing in the opinions of those who would leave the concerns of a religious community to fluctuation and uncertainty; for, besides the constant disadvantages attendant upon mutable and inconstant measures, much danger is to be apprehended from disunion on the one hand, and still more from declension on the other. On this principle it is that we make rules, and establish a discipline calculated to give them proper effect. Precisely on the same ground I would have everything relating to the government of the Church—to the connexion betwixt the Conference and the trustees, and betwixt the Conference, trustees, and people—all definite, substantial, and satisfactory. . . . In giving ours (our Connexion) a legal constitution, I would have our leading principles solemnly recognised; the whole system defined; every privilege secured; all interests consulted; and the whole perpetuated to the latest posterity. I would have this important measure adopted with the knowledge of all parties, with a jealous regard to the interests of all parties, and with the cordial approbation of all parties; that so we may be *one* in heart, interest, and exertion, both now and for ever."*

To supply this desideratum to the Connexion, Mr. Ridgway early set himself to work. He collected information, devised plans, consulted legal advisers. Friends were conferred with, some yielding assent, others expressing fear. The project was at length brought before Conference. Interpreted, not by its own merits and design, but by vague apprehensions of some intentional or possible infringement of ecclesiastical right or privilege, it was virtually rejected. A measure was feared that would centralize the whole authority of the Denomination in a body of men chosen by themselves; whereas the design was to give to the Denomination a legal standing, and thereby

* *Apology*, &c., p. 36.

to provide for the legal defence, and so, of course, for the perpetuity of its principles. It is difficult to argue against fear, still more so against prejudice. Both had to be overcome, and time was required for the victory. The project was broached again, expounded and enforced with all its author's zeal and ability. Again was it defeated, and even decried. Quietly was the deed, prepared with so much care, and at no small personal cost, taken home to be kept for a season more convenient. Reflection succeeded to opposition. Intelligence gained upon prejudice, and confidence upon fear. The need of the rejected measure began to be felt as a safeguard against fluctuation and instability in the institutions of the Connexion. The desire for it spread, and in Mr. Ridgway's own mind acquired additional strength. He gave himself to its furtherance with renewed effort, and, with a firmer hope, as well as with a fuller information, placed it once more before the view of Conference. The right time had now come. His purpose was understood, and his labours were appreciated. Opposition there still was, but this was overborne by the much more general agreement; and shortly afterwards the instrument now known as the Poll Deed was adopted, as a charter giving to the Connexion and its institutions all the sanctity and security of English law.

The *Apology* itself, from which the extract introducing the preceding paragraph is taken, was at the time a service rendered to the Connexion not more seasonable than valuable. It is vigorously written, containing much information and thought, expressed in language condensed and felicitous. It has been succeeded by other publications of the same kind, which have displaced it; let us hope by the last, because by the last occasion for such. It answered an important purpose when it appeared; it could answer no useful purpose now to make it, in any further account, to re-appear. I will therefore content myself with a single quotation from it, expressing one main ground of the author's high appreciation of the polity of the Church to which he belonged. " Amongst many excellencies, this, in my humble opinion," says Mr. Ridgway, "particularly recommends the system of the New Connexion, *that it possesses within itself the elements of purity and reformation.* Those who are acquainted with Church history well know that corruptions have invariably begun in the executive or head, thence descending through all the members. An arbitrary hierarchy will rarely reform itself. . . . . . But if a system be a mixed one, wherein the people have a proper participation, it will correct its errors and reform its abuses. Thus though, like other systems, it is liable to get wrong, still it cannot degenerate, or remain wrong, but will purge itself, according to the power within it, from the evil it has suffered; and by this means not only retain its purity, but rise superior to every obstacle."*

Mr. Ridgway was not much given to authorship. This demanded a process too slow in a region too meditative for his taste. He was a man of action rather than of thought, while yet his acting was the carrying out of thoughts most distinctively his own. Still, his was "the pen of a ready writer." Few have blotted more paper than he. His pen seemed the medium through which he thought; a part almost of himself. Whether in private or in public, in business or other meetings, if not engaged in speaking, he was sure to be engaged in writing. Nor was the paper he blotted wholly a blot, nor only the passing register of things to be immediately attended to, but in many instances the record of reflections which were designed to be read by others. I have before me, in his own hand, a list of twenty-three subjects on which he

* *Apology*, p. 37, *note*.

contributed papers to the *Connexional Magazine*, a number of them running through several successive issues, and some of them afterwards appearing in a separate form. A few of the titles may be given. "A Solemn Warning to those who Love Pleasure more than God;" "Cruelty to Animals Reprobated;" "St. Paul's Visit to Athens;" "God's Sovereignty;" "Thoughts on Toleration;" "Lancasterian System of Education;" "Sabbath Morning Meditation;" "Danger of Lukewarmness;" "Necessity of Perseverance;" "Inducements to Prayer;" "Advice on the Performance of Religious Duties;" "On the Commencement of the New Year;" "Review of the Connexion." The last of these appeared in the year 1815, and was subsequently published, as we have seen, under the title of *An Apology*, &c. The others ranged over periods from that date backward to the year 1807. They were followed by a number of similar contributions, some of which I have been unable to procure or to identify.

When the Church he loved so much required such help, Mr. Ridgway was ready with the service of pen, or tongue, or purse, or all combined. There came a time when all were required in an unusual degree. From without the Connexion had rest. Its day of adversity, of trial that threatened its existence, of embarrassment that crippled its energies, was nearly passed. It had stood firm against shocks from enemies; would it be equally firm against assaults from friends? The storm that had roared in the shrouds had all but died away; what if mutiny should seize the crew, or insidious treachery one of its chiefs? The polity of the Body had endured the severest proof; could its theology be reckoned on if put to a similar test? It was probably necessary to try this question, that the Body might know whether it had a right to live, or that other evangelical bodies might be assured of its life, as the condition of taking it into a close and permanent fellowship; for it seemed beforehand by no means certain—except, perhaps, to a few sagacious thinkers—that, in a constitution which professed to balance and equalize the powers of preachers and people, such an alliance might not be formed between ministerial unfaithfulness on the one hand, and popular sympathy on the other, as would imperil, if not utterly overthrow, in its purity and integrity, the faith of the entire Community. The question was put, and decisively answered.

One whose course has been erring beyond all

other courses, whose path has been downward to a depth below all other depths, was once amongst its most popular ministers. The Gospel he then was set to preach he now derides; the Christ he then professed to love he now traduces and blasphemes. Farther than he goes, whether in denial or abuse, it seems difficult for any one to go. In him infidelity appears to have found its lowest ground and last result. He is the latest and the worst incarnation of its spirit. Paine was hardly more ribald; Voltaire was hardly more scoffing; neither was less unscrupulous, and neither less malicious. It might have been thought that infidelity such as his would have been impossible in the latter half of the nineteenth century; and so it probably would have been in all save an apostate, and an apostate falling so grievously as he fell. But well is it known, and on principles easily understood, that infidelity, when once embraced, exacts much more of those who have been conspicuous for their profession of Christianity than of those who have never made any profession at all. How indeed shall any comfort in its service be obtained but by a violent opposition that shall blind the eyes and harden the heart, by a fever of passionate hatred, that like a lava stream shall consume the spiritual sense to its very socket, and bury or burn out every trace of the faith that was formerly the joy of the soul?

From what precise theological stand-point the downward course of Mr. B. commenced, I know not, and would not conjecture. Some have charged him with fundamental error, and even with insincerity and treachery, from the beginning. For myself, I have many reasons for thinking that the latter supposition at least is unfounded; some of these connecting themselves not only with what I recollect of a ministry which multitudes flocked to hear, and were delighted to hear, but also with memories of services rendered to myself when little more than a mere boy, of which I must for ever preserve a most grateful impression. Nor is either supposition necessary, as the only possible solution of the problem which his career presents. He may have first fallen into sin, and sin may have found an anodyne in doubt, and doubt may have pushed onward to disbelief. Or, in a moment of unguarded speculation, he may have been carried beyond the attraction of some primary truth, and so have stumbled on, "in wandering mazes lost." The descent is easy when the start is taken; easy, not only because momentum is acquired, but because the path lies open.* One

* The classic reader will call to mind Virgil's familiar lines

may look down with dreamy eyes into a lake whose living waters seem to hold strange converse with him, until, overcome by their witchery, he is tempted to plunge heedlessly in. Let the plunge be made, or even one step from the margin be taken, and the bottom is almost sure to be found. There is a singular fellowship and confraternity in error, by which one mistake involves or draws after it another; as there is an organic wholeness, or rather essential unity in truth, especially in revealed truth, realizing itself in a feeling of complete and settled conviction, in a calm steadiness and equilibrium of well-proportioned and well-satisfied faith, so that if one doctrine be surrendered, the next in relation to it can with difficulty be held, and should that one be a chief and controlling verity, the danger is that the whole, even to the last, will fly off, like planets that have lost their centre, leaving the mind without any positive belief at all.

But whatever the point from which this unhappy wanderer started, wander he did. His

---

in the sixth book of his *Æneid*: "Facilis descensus averni," &c. These were the very words which the individual referred to affixed as a motto to his first published sermon. He has since exemplified the former part of the quotation. May he not realize the latter—"sed revocare gradum . . . hoc opus, hic labor est;" or if he do, may the labour not be too difficult to be finally successful!

errors were soon suspected, but the grounds of the suspicion were at first hardly tangible enough to be shaped into a decisive proof. The proof at length came, and was brought home in direct accusation. The errors, however, were not as yet apparently very serious, and, on the promise of their abandonment, were readily forgiven. The promise was not kept, while other errors, affecting not the discipline of the Connexion, as the former had done, but its very doctrines and ordinances, began to discover themselves. They coloured his discourses, cropped out in his ordinary phraseology, in many forms of implication and covert statement appeared in his publications. It became impossible to retain him, except at a cost infinitely greater than the sacrifice of his ability—unquestionably great—ten thousand times repeated. To preserve the purity of the Connexion's faith, and the authority of the Connexion's law, the offending brother must be cut off. The excision took place, wisely and vigorously, though certainly not too soon. The stroke fell by sympathetic rebound on many others: for by a persuasive eloquence, by many a successful defence of the Christianity he now vilifies against the so-called "socialism" of the day, by unwearied industry and seeming disinterestedness and devotion in several departments of public labour, he had acquired great popular influence. Besides, the occasion of his expulsion was improved into an opportunity of dividing the Community to which he had proved himself so unfaithful. Fluent in speech and expert with pen, speech and pen were unrestingly employed to separate preachers from people, and people from preachers. Ambitious of leadership (ambition had had much to do with his fall), a new association of societies was attempted, into which was sought to be drafted whoever could be induced, and from whatever motive, to join his standard. And many were so induced; but only for a time. The work was not of God; it therefore came to nought, as all work must which He does not own. But the Connexion meanwhile suffered, yet in suffering triumphed. It lost much, but gained more. The loss was such as could be told in a tabular statement, and when so told was large enough to make the heart ache. It rose to nearly one-fourth of the whole membership of the Community, and entailed much privation and perplexity on many portions that were left. The gain could not be thus told, but it was gain of rich and ample compensation for the loss, the gain of reputation, of Connexional self-respect, of faith made dearer by endurance, of friendships made closer by suffering, of stability and permanence made surer by trial crowned with conquest—the gain of larger, richer, riper experience in all that makes a church strong, united, influential for every real purpose for which a church exists.

At this crisis many did nobly, rich and poor, ministers and people. Some put forth extraordinary exertion, and not a few made sacrifices even to the point of positive privation. It was a time for prudent counsel and firm determination, a time for rigorous economy, yet generous contribution, a time for all the ability that could be coined into service, whether of tongue or of pen. It was a time therefore peculiarly favourable to the display of Mr. Ridgway's practical talents, and to which their exercise was freely devoted. He had once esteemed, admired, commended the man who was the cause of the present disaster, but now his whole concern was to limit and arrest the mischief. His own circuit was suffering severely, for there this individual had met with much popular favour, and there, for obvious reasons, special efforts were made to produce disaffection and division. The disaffection was widespread, and the division painfully large; for there, as elsewhere, a belief was encouraged, that personal jealousy, and not "corruption from the simplicity that is in Christ," was the motive for the excision that had taken place. All

Mr. Ridgway's energy, eloquence, tact, generosity, reconciling spirit, and local influence, were called into requisition to meet the crisis; and all were offered with a heartiness that meant success, and with a hopefulness that could anticipate no other result. But far beyond his own circuit Mr. Ridgway's concern went out, and far beyond this the effect of his example and labours was felt. His tongue, his pen, his purse, were laid under heavy contribution, and the service of each was given ungrudgingly. The ablest ministers of the Connexion had to confront the adversary, or, in his absence, but in presence of his friends, or of those whose sympathy with him was a fluctuating and irresolute feeling, to defend the acts which had dismembered him from the Body. On many a platform Mr. Ridgway was at their side doing the same thing; as also in many a meeting for deliberation and prayer, in which, while human expedients were devised, the Divine blessing upon them was sought. A periodical was commenced, as an antidote to a similar periodical on the other side, or rather as an answer to a whole flood of publications, in which the most unscrupulous misrepresentation of facts kept fitting company with a germinant heresy, destined to expand into a shocking infidelity. To this Mr. Ridgway was, if not the most frequent, yet one of the ablest contributors.* Liberal gifts were demanded to meet the large and accumulating deficiencies which defection and separation had occasioned to all the funds of the Connexion; and though in this, as in some similar instances, the ministers took the lead, Mr. Ridgway was quick to follow, and to become the leader of multitudes more. In truth, his activity was manifold and unceasing. With his might he did whatsoever his hand found to do, and his hand found much. In various forms and in many places his influence was put forth, and availingly; now by counsel, when perplexities embarrassed; now by gifts, often secretly made, when necessities were urgent; now by friendly visits, when an interview would serve; now by conciliatory offices, when reconciliation was to be effected; always and incessantly by a correspondence which was large enough to be one man's chief anxiety, and which made him as a living presence throughout no small part of the entire Connexion. Here is a specimen of his correspondence at this critical juncture, which I give because, written to a very young man, whom he had never seen, and almost at the beginning of his ministry, it illustrates, by a special example, the statement just made.

* This periodical was commenced and edited, and many of the articles in it written, by the Rev. J. H. Robinson, now superintendent of the Canadian Mission.

"Cauldon Place, Dec. 7th, 1841.

"My dear Sir,—I am concerned to learn that some unpleasant feeling has been occasioned in —— by *the course you have taken* in reference to one or two matters which I need not particularize. Far be it from me to impute blame to you. My worthy informant has not done so, but the contrary. Why then should I do it? I do it not. But I take it some harm has been done, and I suppose is doing. Cannot this be done away with? Pray consult with your excellent friend and superintendent, and try. Our friends are many of them young, and inexperienced in the way. They want things *to be made plain to them;* in short, *to be fed and led*, and treated *with much prudence and forbearance.* You will not regret treating them so in these tickle times, when those who are strong are called to bear the infirmities of the weak, and not to please themselves. I commend the matter to you for Christ's sake, and for the sake of the cause, recommending to you the utmost conciliation and explanation; in short, everything, save what would be sinful, or would lead to sin. I am very desirous that you should hold up your heads, and do well in ——. Please turn your attention to the subject, and let me know how you are going on, and how you succeed in healing this little breach; and when I see you, as I hope to do next month,

I trust we may congratulate one another that the storm, if it deserve the name, has subsided, and that all is love, and joy, and peace.

"Believe me, dear Sir,

"To remain yours truly,

"JOHN RIDGWAY."*

By many Mr. Ridgway will be remembered best and most familiarly as chairman of public meetings, especially public religious meetings. In this capacity his ability, as also his adaptability, was most conspicuous and striking. Such meetings are a distinctive characteristic of our times, and have become frequent almost to excess. They are the outgrowth of public opinion and of public spirit. They are at the same time the means to this, tending to perpetuate and foster that which demands and gives rise to them. When a few thought for the many, as though the many were made for the few—when princes ruled by "right divine," without regard to any

---

* If in the above sketch I have said little or nothing of the labours of others at the time referred to, it is not that I am insensible of their value, but that my purpose was not to write a full account of this episode in our Denominational history, but only so much of it as would serve for general information in connexion with my particular subject. To some, especially to some ministers, living and dead, a debt of gratitude is owing, which the generation now coming into the place of the generation fast passing away, will find it difficult to estimate, if indeed any estimate should ever be thought of.

other right as springing from the people, and therefore very much as suited their own desire— when virtually the only relation which subsisted between the governors and the governed was that expressed by the terms lord and vassal; public opinion there was none, and public meetings there could not well be. Both are the offspring of trade, commerce, education, the diffusion of intelligence and wealth, that whole sum of qualities and conditions which the single word civilization so conveniently represents. In our day, and in this country, these meetings are numerous to satiety, and almost to evil. Yet who would limit their number, or, at least, restrain the liberty to hold them? Such restriction may suit the meridian of St. Petersburg or Vienna, or even be deemed prudent in a city much nearer home; but with us the attempt to impose it would be alike foolish and fruitless. Even license here is better than a compulsory limitation. The free expression of the popular voice is, while a proof that our institutions themselves are free, a means of their improvement and a security for their permanence.

Public religious meetings are the offspring of a public religious spirit. They are also, as in the more general case, the stimulant and nurse of it. They come, not only from the ordinary desire of

Christian fellowship, but from that awakened consciousness of Christian duty in which the great religious organizations of the last century took their rise. Growing out of this, they are eminently serviceable, and, as human nature now is, all but necessary to its continuance; since all voluntary enterprises for the spiritual improvement of our race, involving large gifts and labour, seem to require, because of our native selfishness and sluggishness, the advantage of public association, and the excitement of special appeal. They are thus the sign of the Church's life, of its loyalty to its Head, and of its sympathy for the world; the proof of what is now doing, and the means to a still further work. It is useless to say that in a higher condition of spiritual progress such means will not be necessary. No condition can well be imagined when they will not for some reasons be desirable. And certain it is, whatever sneers a worldly press or an infidel policy may now and then direct to Exeter Hall, the great meetings annually held there for the promotion of Christian objects, and as yearly festivals of societies established to represent them, are among the grandest characteristics of our times. They are as spring blossom, in tropical luxuriance, of the Christian spirit of these latter days.*

* If this cannot be said of the meetings, it may surely be

Mr. Ridgway had great delight in public meetings. He lived almost as much in public as in private. He was not without a certain love of popularity, which these gratified. He had much more of public spirit, which these nurtured, and of which they served as the organ. In his own locality, meetings for religious or educational purposes, on ground neutral to all denominations, not seldom on ground restrictive and peculiar, enjoyed his frequent and never feeble advocacy. In his own denomination, not locally alone but Connexionally, he acquired a character for chairmanship which is not likely to be soon rivalled. Though always an effective, sometimes a really eloquent speaker, one became so much accustomed to see him in the chair, and the chair and he

said of the societies. Think of the following facts. The principal Missionary Societies of this country number at least 7,000 agents and 210,000 communicants, and have together an annual income of more than half a million sterling. The Bible Society is not sixty years old, and yet its receipts this year, 1862, amount to £168,443. Through its means the sacred scriptures have by translations, &c., been made accessible to six hundred millions of our race. The London Society alone sends out yearly 1,787,000 copies of the blessed Book. Then the Tract Society, again, has from sales and contributions an annual income of £95,000. It publishes tracts in 117 languages, and has issues amounting yearly to 21,407,803. What an amount of Christian activity and benevolence, and, after every reasonable abridgment, of Christian usefulness, do these prodigious figures represent!

seemed to have acquired such mutual fitnesses, that each appeared out of place where the other was not.

The office is not so easy to fill, if more be meant for it than a contrivance for announcing the name of speakers, or a bodily presence just up to the mark of asking yes or no to resolutions which a meeting is commonly supposed to adopt. It may almost be said of a chairman as of a poet, that he is born, not made. The making certainly depends very much on the birth. Especially is this true when popular assemblies have to be presided over, and jaded subjects to be enlivened, with indifferent speakers for the task. I suppose, since so many have said so, that a chairman must be, not what Ben Jonson calls a "manling," but a real, full-grown man, of large and noble build; for which reason, possibly it is, that a chair is usually provided for him of more than common capacity. Perhaps the necessity for this arises from the fact that he is the meeting impersonated, and the meeting likes to think well of itself. For a similar reason he must not be too grave, nor at all severe or saturnine, as though he were a judge and not a chairman; not stammering or rude in speech, nor awkward or ungentle in manner; or the meeting might hardly be pleased with such a representation of itself, and would probably decline to acknowledge in his person the reflection of its own spirit. He must rather be friendly and good-humoured; easy and graceful in mood and mien; in hearty sympathy with the occasion, and apt to fit himself into it; able to speak when speaking is needed, and willing to be silent when other speaking should be heard; having withal, as the solid groundwork of all other qualifications, a weight of character and reputation which claims authority by the very respect it ensures. These, in whole or part, are the qualities which the popular idea demands in a chairman; and these, in sober truth, when had in some fair proportion, are ordinarily of great effect in raising the tone of an assembly to at least the pitch of a pleasurable excitement.

These were certainly the qualities possessed by Mr. Ridgway, and which made his chairmanship, especially on occasions of more than ordinary interest, a thing to be afterwards remembered. If he rose to speak, as he sometimes did, with an air which a stranger might call stately, or an unfriendly critic self-important, he never failed to command respect either for his position or himself; and rarely did he fail to touch the key to which the subsequent proceedings were or should be harmonized. He sat or stood as one made to preside, and so used his authority, rather perhaps his opportunity, that compliance and approval became much more a pleasure than either a formality or a task. Grave or gay, lively or severe, he was with quick transition, and could be almost so at will, assuredly with most easy and pliant adaptation. If the occasion was a serious one, particularly if one of unusual interest and importance, he was not content nor expected to be content with the expression of a few introductory or apologetic commonplaces, but plunged leader-like into the very heart of the question which was uppermost in the thoughts of all present, and sometimes—increasing in volume of voice and rapidity of utterance as he went along, striking fire from his short, crisp, burning sentences, like an impassioned steed in full course, with flushed countenance and heavy movement of his whole body—wrought himself and those who heard him up to a pitch of almost unmanageable excitement. If the occasion were more friendly and familiar—one of those social gatherings which in these days of popular comings together mark the commencement or signalize the conclusion of some special enterprise for the Church's weal, in which many heads and hands have been or are to be employed,—or one of those annual assemblies connected with a society or denomination to which, interested in each other and in some purpose and object common to them all, people come for kindly fellowship, and refreshment of their spirits by exercises which serve—while for general relaxation and holiday festivity—for religious instruction and enjoyment, as well as for stimulus and encouragement in the particular ends to be pursued and furthered, he became, as the phrase ordinarily is, though with more than the ordinary truth, the life of the whole meeting, suffusing and pervading it with his own full, fresh, cheery, exuberant spirit. He had the faculty of putting every one, speaker and hearer, into good humour, and of sustaining the agreeable excitement to the close. He knew how to be silent when others, on any substantial grounds, had claims to be listened to; but in the absence of such the interest of the hour was seldom allowed to flag. Rarely could any one come from a meeting over which he presided and speak of it as unprofitable or dull. If the net result was nothing positive that could be consciously added to other accumulated treasure to be used in future, it was at least something pleasant, of which the memory to-morrow would be no worse than the enjoyment to-day. He could be humorous or grave, as the feeling was, or the subject demanded; sometimes, however, passing from one mood to the other with a swiftness which in most would have seemed startling, but in him was felt to be natural. He was seldom at a loss for a fitting remark, where a single remark would suffice; for a delicate compliment, or a good-humoured joke, and especially for that happy, instantaneous wit, which conceals—behind a sly reference—a *double entendre*, a felicitous pleasantry, or a real practical lesson.

Of this many instances will be in the recollection of those who have heard him often, but all, from the want of those circumstantial accessories which give point and freshness to such stories, would lose in the telling. Of the delicate compliment, the following, though given in private, may be taken as a specimen. Dr. Raffles, of Liverpool, was several times Mr. Ridgway's guest. On one of these occasions, the Doctor, observing his own portrait suspended immediately above another portrait which he did not at the moment recognise, inquired whose it was. "Ah!" replied his host, "it may be presumption to place myself so near to you; but you see, Doctor, I am content to sit at your feet."

Another instance, of a somewhat different kind —of wit looking in several directions, and suggesting much more than it expressed—occurred at a congregational meeting, which took place but a few days before his death, of which meeting the recollection remained with him as more than a common joy. I give it here, in preference to any other, though he was not himself on this occasion the chairman, mainly for the reason just stated; because, that is, it was among the last of such instances, and was connected in his own mind, as well as in the minds of others, with endearing memories of an unusually happy evening. The meeting was presided over by his friend Mr. Love, and was got up partly for congratulation on the success of very strenuous and praiseworthy exertions put forth by a small number of friends to build a new and handsome chapel, and to establish a new church; and partly for encouragement and enterprise to pursue the work to its completion, by freeing the chapel from debt and filling the pews yet vacant with hearers. Towards the former Mr. Love, though not locally connected with the place, had lent some assistance, and now promised to lend more. But there had been uneasiness and strife in the congregation and church, occasioned by certain disciplinary acts in respect to individuals who were not without power to do harm. The case has no interest now, but it excited much at the time, and far beyond its legitimate sphere. Its whole history was known to Mr. Ridgway; so was the better history of the little band of people to found a new church, which had terminated so successfully. Warmed by the promises of the chairman, as also by a Report which contained many congratulatory references to the past, the meeting became excited. One speaker after another took up the note of commendation, pitching his address to the key of the Report. "The chapel," it was said, "had been built in Faith and sustained by Faith." The sentiment was handed from each to the next, and repeated again and again. Mr. Ridgway rose at the call of the chairman, and with brimming animation began: "Well, my friends, it is all very well to talk about Faith, but I can't help thinking (seizing the chairman by the arm), that in this instance Faith has worked by LOVE," adding, with a countenance of roguish humour which it was a real enjoyment to see, "I'll say nothing about its purifying the heart." At this meeting, it may be here added, his long life of service for the Connexion as a public speaker, away from his own home, was brought to a close. And by many it was observed how mellowed and chastened his spirit was, how deep and exquisite his religious enjoyment. His feeling, ever strong as a spring tide, yet mostly under the repression of a sovereign will, fairly broke loose and ran over in tears when the congregation sang, "There shall be no more sorrow there."

: CHAPTER V.

The Labourer in the Vineyard.

CHAPTER V.

THE LABOURER IN THE VINEYARD.

In the preceding chapter, Mr. Ridgway appears principally in what I may call his denominational character. As belonging to some section of the Church universal, every Christian man must have a character of this kind, who has any ecclesiastical preferences at all. Happily there are but few whose preferences take any other expression than that of a quiet adherence to the polity of the church in the faith and worship of which their fathers trained them, or by the ministry of which they have been brought into the common fellowship of the Gospel. Were it otherwise, the polemical spirit would know but little rest and scarcely any bounds, and the fever of agitation and controversy, invading the sacred retreats and sanctuaries of personal and social piety, would dry up, as a hot sun the tender herb, those sweet and gentle charities which come forth in their prime only in the vivifying atmosphere of a daily communion with God. Still, preferences there are and must be, and occasions will arise when these demand a bold and unmistakable expression. But only a few are ever called upon, as only a few are competent, especially without injury to their higher spiritual interests, to take any part openly and decisively in asserting or defending them; and these few, from their very position as leaders, are sure to acquire a certain denominational character which all but overlays, and in some cases so completely overlays as to render invisible, the broader character which belongs to them as followers of Jesus Christ. Yet, how much better, nobler, every way worthier is the one character than the other? It sounds but as a mere platitude or truism, while yet the remark acquires now and then a special significance, to say, that it is of little consequence for a man to belong, with whatever zeal of partisanship, to any particular ecclesiastical establishment, or even to render much outward estimable support to any one single church, considered simply as a church, and especially as a rival to any other church.

His real Christian worth is apart from all this, or only so much in connexion with it that this is but the visible manifestation—under those conditions of human imperfection which ever mar that which is best in us—of something which is far higher and better. "What doth the Lord require of thee," demands the prophet, "but to do justly, and to love mercy, and to walk humbly with thy God?" Where this requirement is not fulfilled, and fulfilled in that higher spiritual sense which all divine precepts have acquired under the Gospel, the will of God has yet to be done; and where this is not done, whatever denominational attachment is evinced, nothing is done.

Nor is that a healthful or expansive piety which restricts itself in sympathy to one particular church, so as to be able to rejoice in its prosperity alone, or, if in the prosperity of other churches, yet with a joy so rebuked and saddened by envy, that it is hardly any joy at all. Nor, again, is that a high Christian activity which, with rare gifts—of wealth, intellect, social position—finds no sphere, and desires none beyond the inclosure of its own chosen denomination, but almost always steadfastly resists the application for help that could easily be rendered on the plea, variously modified, that "charity begins at home." Hardly different is this from the spirit of the disciples who, when they saw one whom they did not recognise as of their company casting out devils, forbade him, though he did the work in the name of their Master; "because," such was their excuse, "he followeth not us." And very much allied is it to that narrowness which the first Christian emperor is said to have rebuked in Acesius, the Novatian, who, when the latter would restrict the terms of communion to the peculiarities of his own sect, replied in the words, "Ho! Ho! Acesius; plant a ladder, and climb up into heaven by yourself."*

Of Mr. Ridgway it was said, and published immediately after his death, "Never did a father cherish a stronger affection for his only son than did our dear friend for the Connexion." The remark is broadly true, and even the illustrative comparison, though somewhat extreme, may in the main be admitted, if by father be understood one who has room enough in his heart for more than his own family, and by Connexion be meant less an organization for the maintenance of some form of ecclesiastical polity than an association of churches for the furtherance and spread of pure

* Stanley's *Eastern Church*, 175.

and undefiled religion. Mr. Ridgway was very far from what is known as bigotry, though sufficiently precise and definite in all his religious views. He was not a sectary, otherwise than as any one belonging by intelligent preference, and especially by conspicuous and influential adhesion, to any particular Christian Society is this. A broad common sense, pervaded and directed by an equally broad and diffusive charity, carried him beyond the prejudices which mostly circumscribe our sympathies, and gave him an interest, real and practical, in the well-being of other denominations than his own. Though a conscientious dissenter, and ever willing at seasonable times to avow and defend his nonconformity, he not only maintained a friendly intercourse with clergymen and members of the Establishment, but was ready with his help in their work, when help could be honourably given and received. Before me are letters from clergymen acknowledging such help, and bearing testimonies to his personal worth. "I highly esteem," says one, "the catholic spirit in which you have made this donation, and am fully prepared to acknowledge 'catholicity' of this description to be 'one of the notes of the true church.'" "I had the pleasure of knowing him well for many years," says another, farther away from his own home, "and of acting with him in various matters, both civil and religious. I always found him disposed to that which is most liberal and Christian. I deeply regret his decease; I feel it a loss to me personally, for though we differed in some things, we cordially agreed in those things which are essential to the salvation of men and to the glory of God. It is, however, a very serious loss to the Church of Christ in this neighbourhood in general, and to his part of it in particular." The spirit of the Evangelical Alliance was eminently his spirit, falling in with that "peace-loving disposition" which was natural to him, but which Christianity had exalted into a religious sentiment; and long before the body called by that name had sprung into existence, as also long after, he found in the objects and proceedings of the Bible Society, of which society he was for many years the local president, the means of commending this spirit to others, and of fostering it in himself. "Mr. Ridgway's spirit was as catholic as it was Connexional," says one who resided very near to him. "All good men and all evangelical communities he admired and loved, and was ever ready to help them, either by his presence or his purse. For many years his name stood on the list of subscribers to the Bible Society, the Evangelical Alliance, the Moravian, Baptist,

London, and Wesleyan Missionary Societies, and on that connected with many other educational and philanthropic institutions in this district; while, as chairman of innumerable public meetings, no man seemed so popular and ubiquitous as he."

In his own church Mr. Ridgway's religious activity—his activity not only as a "ruling elder" concerned for its discipline, but as a devout member, anxious for its edification and increase —was incessant and multiform. He bore its spiritual interests perpetually on his heart. Its life mingled with his own life. He knew as if by vital sensibility, assuredly by intimate fellowship and habitual devotion to appointed means of grace, its true spiritual condition. He thought of it daily, and thought of it much. Few enjoyed its privileges as he; none had more concern for its welfare. If he went from home, Bethesda went with him. He could not forget it, and did not wish. If his stay was prolonged, he must be kept informed of its state. His mind turned to it as though by magnetic attraction: its hours of service, whether public or private, in the sanctuary or the class-room, calling up as they returned refreshing memories of the past, and awakening ardent longings for the future. When the cause of God languished, or appeared to languish, his soul was disquieted within him; when it prospered, its prosperity was as a new personal blessedness. Only in rare cases do we find such a complete identification of the church and the individual as was witnessed in him. His was the love which could say, "If I forget thee, O Jerusalem, let my right hand forget her cunning. . If I prefer not Jerusalem above my chief joy."

It was hence a privilege to him to work, to work much and in many ways for the improvement and enlargement of the church. He did not, like some rich men, satisfy himself with giving, as though that were a full discharge of duty, or a sufficient equivalent for other men's labour. He counted his talents too accurately, and weighed his responsibility too conscientiously, for that. He laboured himself, esteemed it an honour to labour, enjoyed the work above all other work. There are few, if any, among the many spheres of practical usefulness which Methodism provides for its members, which at one time or other he did not fill,—and fill, not by routine performance of ceremony, but by earnest discharge of duty. He could not feebly do anything. Whatever he undertook, he went through with his might. He was a class leader and local preacher to the last. In the former capacity he had, for a long series of years, done much and gained much. The opportunities of Christian intercourse it furnished were dear to him. He had no reluctance to pour out his soul before others, united in the same selected fellowship. He liked the dealing with himself, the close grappling with his own conscience, the faithful review of the past which the occasion demanded; the calm retreat from the world, the answering of heart to heart, as face to face in a glass, which the occasion afforded. Yet not for enjoyment more than for usefulness did he use the office. Those intrusted to his care were cared for with pastoral tenderness, visited in sickness, counselled in difficulty, helped in need, thought of, as we shall afterwards see, when he was far away, nor forgotten—such as required to be remembered—in the provisions of his last will. The office was a means of edifying others, and he used it for this object; of enlarging the church, and he honoured it to this end. "Sir," said he to a gentleman whom he had invited one Sabbath evening to the house of God, and who he saw had been wrought upon by the word preached, "I am a recruiter for King Jesus; and I now invite you to meet me on Wednesday evening at the class of which I have the honour to be the leader."

To the fact of Mr. Ridgway's preaching I have

referred before, though to little more than the fact. He belonged, and this by clear conviction of duty, to that numerous and important body of Christian workers known as lay or local preachers, who in Methodist societies from the beginning, and now in some other societies, are engaged as auxiliaries to the regular ministry; and to whose labours, voluntarily and gratuitously rendered, the growth of religious denominations in this country, and so also the spread of religion itself, is in no small measure to be attributed. In his appearance there was little which, according to any familiar type, could be called clerical. He was rather a model of "the fine old English gentleman," stately and mannerly, with a full, round countenance, brimming, in his best mood, with a cheerful good-nature. The toll-gate keeper —a woman—was therefore not to be blamed, judging from his looks, in refusing to admit his claim to exemption from the usual tax, on the plea that he was going to the neighbouring village to preach. "Nay, nay," said the feminine physiognomist, "yo munna deceive me; yo've too merry a face to be a parson." With a merry face, he had also a merry heart at times, but always a very serious one in the service of his Master.

At one time he preached much, and acquired

no small popularity as a preacher. He preached to the close of his life, with no abatement of energy, but with an increase of unction which betokened the deeper impression of eternal things on his own heart. When civil honours came thick upon him, he still preached, adjudging that the civil and the sacred were by no means incompatible; carrying the former into the latter for their better consecration, and giving to the latter the benefit of whatever influence the former had to bestow. Not very long before he died he went to a small town about a dozen miles from his home to fulfil an appointment there. The chapel was an extremely humble one, and the church was a new mission which he with others had taken some pains to establish. His name attracted attention, and drew some gentlemen of the neighbourhood to hear him. One, a wealthy magistrate, at the close of the service, complimented him on his condescension in coming to preach to the people. "Sir," replied Mr. R., "I do no honour to the work; the work honours me. You too, sir, are as much bound to serve Christ and preach His Gospel as I am; and it would do you honour too, sir, allow me to say, and would give you a joy the world can never give." This reply, towards the end of his Christian career, when age, like the first slight frost of deepening autumn, had barely signalled the coming in of wintry decline, was worthy of that earlier rebuke in which, when comparatively young, he said to certain "respectables" who had taunted him with being a Methodist:—"Gentlemen, I am choosing my companions for eternity."

Mr. Ridgway, I have said, was characteristically a man of action rather than of thought. His thoughts came rapidly when at all. They were, at least what was best in them, the immediate offspring of his feeling — generated in a moment, thrown off at a heat. He had nothing carefully prepared, nor anything prepared at all, but the merest outline. His anxiety was to prepare himself, and then to trust to the excitements and suggestions of the occasion; or rather, perhaps, in some degree of personal fitness for such communications, to expect from above the helps vouchsafed to those who need and wait for them. His sermons, therefore, were not studies, but addresses; not doctrinal discussions, but practical appeals. Intensely practical they were; clear and forcible in their exposition of truth when truth was to be expounded, but even sharp and ringing in expression, pithy and pointed in separate sentences, glowing with the fire of his kindling passion, and directed like well-aimed bolts at the hearts of his hearers. Effectiveness was hence the characteristic of his preaching. His earnestness was contagious. His hearers could not be indifferent while listening to him. He was sure to impress where he did not convince; and godly and ungodly alike, having heard him once, were wishful to hear him again.

No complete specimens can be given, and if any could, as to their matter, these would want the force and vividness of his manner. Of sermons, properly so called, he has left none behind him; of notes, drafts, outlines, a tolerably large collection; though all of them apparently belonging to an early period of his life. These have little merit in themselves, as, indeed, outlines prepared by abler hands than his seldom have much; but those who knew him, and who read these pages to freshen their recollections of what he was and what he did, will be interested to read a small selection. The following are taken almost at random, and are examples of dozens more.

"Acts ix. 11. *For, behold, he prayeth.* Introduce with Paul's history and conversion, then proceed to describe—

"I. THE CHARACTER AND DUTY OF PRAYER.— Prayer is the breathing of the desire, the language of the soul. It requires not set words; the thought, the eye, the heart,—all may pray. It is addressed to God, a spiritual Being—comes from spiritual feelings, therefore sincere, earnest, fervent. It is for blessings which none can grant but He. It is regulated by His Word, and according to His will. It must be believing, through Christ, with reliance on His gracious promises. Is the duty of all; what all may engage in. Must be public, must be social, must be family,—but, most of all, must be private. Such was the prayer of Saul of Tarsus.

"II. Its SEASONABLENESS.—It is becoming and profitable under all circumstances. The morning light; the evening repose; daily mercies; family blessings; petition for the Church; supplication for all men. But there are peculiar seasons when of all others it is most necessary and useful. As in forming our plans for life; in entering upon new connexions; in journeying from home; in the time of affliction; in the day of poverty and distress; in the hour of provocation and temptation; when the soul languishes in gracious feeling and in religious exercise; when inclined to depart from God and His people; when worldly feelings prevail to the injury of heavenly; when the cause of God declines and needs reviving. But most of all our text refers to the awakened sinner into whose soul divine light has darted, who is arrested as it were by the hand of God; wounded by the law; softened by the Gospel; shocked at himself; terrified at God; alarmed at the prospect before him; no hope, no safety in anything; but driven or drawn to Calvary, to the throne of grace, with streaming eyes, bended knees, heart humbled, and hands uplifted—then, indeed, may it be said, 'Behold, he prayeth.' Oh, brethren, many of you know all this; you recollect the time with joy and gratitude. And all may know and feel it; all must know and feel it. And this is the accepted time. And have you any objection, my fellow-sinners, to enjoy the same blessings, &c. &c. Let me remind you that the day of affliction, of dissolution, is a time for prayer; the day of judgment will be too late.

"III. THE ADVANTAGES OF THIS CONDUCT.— We please God by honouring His command, acknowledging our dependence, doing our duty. We gain blessings for ourselves when we most need them, viz., when no one can help but God only, especially at that critical time when the spirit is striving, Christ is willing, angels waiting, saints desiring our salvation. On prayer then our conversion, our peace, our happiness may depend. Prayer is full of blessings throughout our Christian course; and at that awful period when heart and flesh fail. Prayer is the means of blessing to our families, to the Church, to the world. Sinners are saved by it, good men and angels rejoice, devils fear and tremble, and God the Father, Son, and Spirit, are well pleased, and unite in bestowing blessings.

"My young friends, can it be said of any of you, 'Behold, he prayeth'? Middle-aged, is it possible that any of you have not yet begun to pray? Sinner, it is high time to begin, &c. Humble seeker, with such encouragement will you not, &c. Believer, this is your happiness and privilege, &c. &c. Then pray more and more, continue in prayer till prayer is lost in praise, &c. &c."

"John iii. 14. *And as Moses lifted up the serpent in the wilderness, even so must the Son of man be lifted up: that whosoever believeth in Him should not perish, but have eternal life.* It is most pleasing to see the truths of the New Testament illustrated by those of the Old, and those of the Old confirmed by those of the New. This text is founded on an event which occurred in the journey of Israel through the wilderness. They were led by a pillar of cloud by day and of fire by night, protected by Almighty power, fed by bread from heaven, and with water from the flinty rock; yet they murmured against the Lord, until His anger was kindled against them. The serpents of the desert were sent to sting and destroy them. Those who escaped their deadly bite were in danger from the more deadly plague.

Terror and death were in the camp of Israel. The people humbled themselves before Moses and the Lord, and supplicated for deliverance. Immediately the man of God stood in the gap, and prayed for the people. The God of mercy and of Israel heard and answered: 'Make thee a fiery serpent,' &c. &c. (Numbers xxi. 8). Moses instantly obeyed. The crisis was awful: the people were dying, the evil spreading, &c. Soon a brazen serpent was made, was raised on a pole; carried, perhaps, through the tents of Israel. Proclamation would doubtless be made; the stung and diseased would be removed to the door of the tent; each darkening eye be directed to the mysterious serpent, and each bosom sob, 'If I can but look, I shall be saved.'

"Oh, what a miracle of mercy and of love! How fully displaying the power and goodness of God! How simple and benevolent the expedient! Adapted to all; trial of faith; means of glorifying God, while saving the sinner.

"And what a lively picture does this event hold out of the dear Redeemer; of His atonement; of the manner in which He is to be held forth to a sinful world; and of the means by which the salvation that is in Him must be had.

"I. THE NECESSITY OF CHRIST'S DEATH.—Laid in the state of man, His fall and consequent misery and danger. In the counsels of God from eternity; in the promises of God in time. In the unbounded love of Jesus Christ. Hear Him say, 'I go to Jerusalem,' &c. It behoved Christ to suffer, &c.

"II. THE GREAT DESIGN OF ALL THIS.—To mark God's displeasure against sin; to exhibit His love and mercy for the sinner; to make redemption honourably consistent with His character and law; to win, by the extent of His grace, the sinner's heart; to save the humble penitent from death, and exalt him to everlasting life. What stupendous love! What a glorious object! What a blissful change! From death to life; from hell to heaven!

"III. THE MANNER IN WHICH THESE BLESSINGS ARE TO BE REALIZED—'That whosoever,' &c. By believing the record which God hath given of them (1 John v. 11). As leading to this, and also as springing from it, by an experimental conviction that we have sinned; are diseased, smitten unto death, from which the mercy of God alone through Christ can deliver us. By an humble, earnest inquiry and seeking. By simple, hearty reliance upon Christ, looking steadfastly upon Him as lifted up, and accepting His salvation as free, full, all-sufficient. All this beautifully pointed out in the case before us. The Israelites had sinned; so have we. The Lord punished with death; and we are under the sentence. Moses interceded, and a remedy was provided. 'Deliver him from going down to the pit,' &c., said the Saviour, and He Himself became our remedy. Means were personally to be used, otherwise the remedy was unavailing; it is thus in our case. The Divine blessing attended the means to make them effectual; so with us. The serpent was to be exalted; so Christ. To be seen; so must He. To be relied on, &c. &c.

"The wonderful manifestation of God in Christ —a manifestation of love. Duty of sinners; of penitents; of believers, to live to and adore Him; of ministers, to present Him, lift Him up, commend Him to view, to admiration, to faith; of all, to prepare to meet Him at His second coming, when His cross shall be exchanged for His crown."

"Matt. xiii. 3—9. *The Parable of the Sower.* Imagine to yourselves the blessed Redeemer as thus presented. He has left the house where He has been teaching; multitudes have followed Him, impelled, no doubt, by different motives. The sea-shore is the place of meeting, a ship His pulpit, the heavens His canopy; compassion in His heart, the glory of His

Father in His eye. It was here the Saviour gave those beautiful parables recorded in this chapter; parables which bespeak His wisdom, representing spiritual things by things temporal, and which, by a wonderful adaptation to every age of the Church and the world, are calculated to instruct poor sinners in divine knowledge, and edify them that believe in the grace of Christ.

"Our text represents a minister of the Gospel under the image of a sower of seed. It describes the Word of God—the Gospel—as seed sown; living seed, precious seed, the everlasting seed of the kingdom. It represents the sower — the minister—going forth to sow; that is, pursuing his daily task of dispensing and scattering heavenly truth. It sets forth the various kinds of soil on which the seed falls—the different dispositions and affections of those who hear the Gospel preached. It shows the diversified results of the operation. The two last will be the subjects of more particular consideration.

"I. THE FIRST CLASS OF HEARERS ARE THOSE ON THE WAYSIDE. Here was no previous cultivation. Here were no fences, no restraints; all was unprotected and open,—a common thoroughfare; the ground trodden, hard, and barren. The seed lies on the surface, will not take root, the fowls devour it; that is, ungodly habits, companions, lusts, &c. &c.

II. THE SECOND CLASS ARE STONY GROUND HEARERS. They have a slight covering of earth, but no depth. Their hearts are susceptible; they hear the Gospel cordially, they even approve it; they form good resolutions, but they do it in their own strength; they do not get the root of the matter—their hearts broken, subdued to penitence, and filled with grace to forsake every evil way. No, no; they beat a parley, they halt, they compromise, seek to serve two masters, retain their lusts, keep back their hearts, cannot therefore stand temptation, evil company, persecution; for want of root, of moisture, the seed wasteth away, the sun scorches it, the soul perisheth.

III. THE THIRD CLASS ARE THE THORNY GROUND HEARERS. These have more soil, and better cultivation. The seed takes root, springs up, flourishes, encourages cheering hopes. Ah! the hopeful prospect is blasted; for thorns grow up and mingle with the tender corn. Such are the cares of the world, the love of riches, the pleasures and fashions of life. Ah, these things cannot be mingled with religion, and religion long survive. They are soon preferred; the heart becomes cold, the desires languish, prayer

M

and other Christian duties are neglected, and the seed sown dies.

IV. THE FOURTH CLASS ARE THE FRUITFUL HEARERS. These are those whose hearts are as good ground, well prepared and cultivated; those who have yielded, and still desire to yield, to influences from above; who are wishful to hear what God shall say; who put away prejudice, &c.; who listen, approve, treasure up; who, under Divine influences, embrace Christ as their Saviour; who bring forth the fruits of good living, of holiness and usefulness, to the glory of God. Not, indeed, all in the same measure, but always of the same kind, in proportion to the grace given and improved. All are saved, though with a salvation different in degree. The Church is blessed, and God is glorified.

IMPROVEMENT. "Who hath ears to hear, let him hear." Let him see the design of the Gospel, the goodness of God in sending it, the purpose of His ministers in proclaiming it, the reason why it is so frequently rejected, why so often unproductive, why so many begin in the spirit and end in the flesh, why also some hear to purpose and produce fruit. In all cases the seed is the same, often the sower the same, always so when Christ is thought of as the sower, and His Gospel as the seed; but oh! how different the result. "He that hath ears to hear, let him hear." Let us bring the matter home to our experience. How have we heard? How neglected? How improved? What are we doing to-day? Attending, approving, professing, working? Nothing short of this will avail. By their fruits ye shall know them: the fruits of repentance, faith, holiness on earth, then will be eternal life in heaven."

A few outlines are longer than these, many shorter, but all present the same general features. Now and then the meaning of a passage is neatly gathered up into several connected propositions, very briefly expressed, as in 1 Timothy i. 15: *"This is a faithful saying, and worthy of all acceptation, that Christ Jesus came into the world to save sinners,"* the thoughts in which are thus given: "I. A Gospel truth. II. A Gospel blessing. III. A Gospel duty." It is unnecessary, however, to amplify these further, or to add to the number of extracts from Mr. Ridgway's papers, as these are sufficient to illustrate, if not the character of his delivered sermons, yet the kind of sketches he made before preaching.

Mr. Ridgway exercised a private as well as a public ministry. This took the form of a correspondence by letter to friends at a distance, whenever counsel might be offered, or consolation could be given. His fertile pen was ever ready with a word in season when the occasion called for it; and because, among so large a number who had intimate relations to him, important changes were always taking place, the occasion was frequently occurring. Still, in the absence of anything very remarkable in his correspondence, two or three specimens will serve to indicate its general characteristics. They all relate to times when kindly remembrances and Christian counsel and sympathy are especially valued. Here is a letter to one, the daughter of an esteemed minister, whom consumption wasted away, while yet the Holy Spirit glorified, before she was twenty years of age.

"Cauldon Place, Oct. 12, 1856.

"My dear Girl (whom I have known and loved ever since we first saw each other), it has affected me much to learn that you are sick, and, to all appearance, about to leave us. This is indeed unexpected, and, I had almost said, unwelcome. But I dare not use that term, for how can it be unwelcome, though we leave parents and friends, to depart and be with Christ, which is far better. God, who has mercifully spared me to do a little more work, turns about in His wisdom and love to take you, because your work is well-nigh done, and His purpose is that you may enter His glory, and be for ever with the Lord. We may and shall mourn our loss, but we dare not desire you to be kept in this world of sin and sorrow, of sickness and sighing, to be kept out of that mansion which the Saviour has gone to prepare for you. Ah, no! it would be too selfish, and we will not do it. You are going home, to happiness, to saints above, to angels, to the Lord who bought you, and to God, your everlasting Father and covenant-keeping Friend, to enter upon a bliss of which we can know nothing equal to it in this world—upon an eternal state whose glories eye hath not seen, nor hath ear heard. Ah, no! we must not attempt to detain you from such delightful company and joys. Our business must be to pray that you may be comforted, and cheered, and sanctified, and fully ripened for the coming of your Lord. I will join dear friends in supplicating the mercy-seat, that your love may be sweeter, your faith stronger, your hope as an anchor—in short, Christ all in all. And we will pray that patience may have its perfect work, the tempter kept at a distance,

> " ' And not a cloud arise,
> To darken the skies,
> Or hide for a moment,
> The Lord from your eyes.'

"Oh, I am thankful that you are standing on

the foundation that God has laid in Zion. What a blessing! Pious parents are a blessing, and a great one. Christian friends and ordinances are great blessings. But religion and a precious Saviour are greater blessings than them all. And this leads me to say, you are going before us, but we are following after, in the same road, and to the same heaven. Every dear child that goes thither, makes heaven more desired and valued by parents; and the same of friends. You will be one more to welcome us; and how happy, my dear young friend, will be our meeting:

" ' Far from a world of grief and sin,
With God eternally shut in !'

"Do not, my dear girl, fear a little more suffering, for your consolation shall abound. Do not fear any stripe, for whom the Lord loves he chastens. Do not fear the last enemy, for he is conquered. Do not fear the silence of the grave, for them that sleep in Jesus, God will bring with Him. Do not fear the Judge, for He is your friend, and will give you His benediction. . . . My dear sufferer, cast yourself on the covenant of grace, and thereby lay fast hold on Christ. Sweetly fall into His hands, and say, 'Not as I will, O Lord, but as Thou wilt.' Submit patiently to His rod, and it will blossom with love. . . . I should be happy to see you, and say farewell for a few short days and months—for we shall soon embrace each other in glory—but this I cannot hope. Thank God, your dear pious father and mother and friends will be always at hand to speak consolation, and their prayers for you will be heard and answered. Above all, around you will be the everlasting arms, and ere long the chariot will be sent, and Jesus bid you come. I send you, my dear girl, my love, prayers, and blessing. God I know will be gracious to you and yours. Your last days will be your best, and, full of longing and happiness, you will leave us, crying, 'Victory,' through the blood of the Lamb. Grant this, God of faithfulness and love, to you and yours, and to me. Even so, Amen.

"I am, my dear girl,
"Most truly and affectionately yours,
"JOHN RIDGWAY."

In less than a month after this the "chariot" *was* "sent," and Eliza Wright mounted it, "singing"—so it is recorded of her—as they only can sing who know that its ultimate destination is the third heaven of God's unspeakable glory. To her deeply afflicted father, the Rev. P. J. Wright, Mr. Ridgway addressed the following consolatory communication:—

"Cauldon Place, Nov. 9, 1856.

"My dear Friend,—The reception of your mournful letter could not surprise me, having been in daily expectation of hearing that all was over, and your angelic daughter gone to the heaven for which she was so happily prepared. God entrusted her to you, and you have now entrusted her to Him. She has gone a little, and but a little, before you; and there will be no disappointment, for you and your dear wife will meet her, and so be for ever with the Lord. She is too happy to wish for a change; and you will only wait for your change, when the end of being will be answered, when your work and service will be done, and the reward, like hers, will be, 'Enter thou into the joy of thy Lord.' You will miss your dear girl much; but the recollection that she has done with sorrow, and suffering, and death, and is now before the throne of God and the Lamb, will lead your thoughts to the same blessedness, and cause you to rejoice in the hope of the glory of God. I pray God to sustain you and your dear partner under this severe bereavement. You must cheer and comfort her, and God will abundantly comfort you. And be not surprised if you love God more, and preach for Him better. Depend upon it, these events have a sanctifying influence on our hearts and lives. So they are designed to have; and my prayer is, that it may be eminently so in your experience,—that you make the decease of your dear girl the beginning of better and brighter days, in all holiness, happiness, and usefulness. . . . . Adieu, my dear friend. God be gracious to you, and lift on yours the light of His countenance, and grant you resignation and peace.

"I am faithfully yours,
"JOHN RIDGWAY."

One other brief note, of like kind. It is addressed to Mr. Heaps, of Leeds, on the death of his father, or rather through him to the whole family of brothers.

"Cauldon Place, Sept. 7, 1856.

"MY DEAR FRIEND,—On my return home yesterday, I met the record of your dear father's death. The event would not be unexpected to you, as it was not to me, I having heard of his approaching end, and you having witnessed the various stages of his decline up to the last. How well I recollect his friendly and amiable countenance for years past and gone! But his frame had been sadly shattered, and even his benevolent eye and intellectual countenance had all undergone a change. But he is released. Disease and death have no more power over him. The sleep will soon be broken, and mortality will be swallowed up of life. And we also shall meet him in that country where is no decay, no sickness, no separation, no death; where God shall wipe away all tears, where the days of our mourning shall be ended, and our happiness shall be complete and eternal. We will not therefore sorrow, nor wish our friends back, but wish rather to follow them, and so to be ever with the Lord. The head is gone. You and brothers must now be all heads. Each go up higher, and live, and serve, and do more than ever. God grant you the ability and the grace! Read these few lines to your dear brothers. I have all of you in high esteem, and every branch of your families. My affectionate regards to them. I pray God to bless you all, and the beloved cause, both in Leeds and everywhere. Can you send me a few lines describing your dear parent's last day and hour? I shall be much obliged. And has he not left a widow? Pray nourish her, and present to her my love and sympathy.

"Believe me, dear Friend,
"To be affectionately and faithfully yours,
"JOHN RIDGWAY."

CHAPTER VI.

Unconscious Self-Portraiture.

CHAPTER VI.

UNCONSCIOUS SELF-PORTRAITURE.

A MAN's real worth, I have said, is apart from his preferential connexion with any particular denomination. It depends not at all on his belonging to this Church or that, and attaches in no necessary way to anything he may outwardly do for its exclusive furtherance and support. It lies rather in that which is strictly personal, as between himself and God; and appears in little things rather than great, in private rather than in public—in the quiet flow of daily existence, that is, in those multitudinous acts connected together by the continuous interest of domestic and social life, which singly are of small importance, but together make up, as sands the mountain and as moments the year, that whole aggregate which we express in the general term character.

A man never is what at particular times he

tries to be. He may not be—sometimes is not—what on great occasions he seems, as the occasion may reflect upon him what belongs rather to itself than to him. But he always is what in private life he seems, what in daily routine of familiar business and quiet service of domestic duty he appears. His true self comes out best where there is least thought of self, when he has no audience to speak to, no spectators to observe him, but moves on in a natural way of self-manifestation, without regard to those about him, save as this regard is required for his own interest or for theirs; speaking because he thinks; feeling because he must; doing because he wills. Both the best and worst part of a man's life, inner and outer, is often that which is secret, which has no witnesses and no record. Perhaps this is always so, even in those cases where individuals have mirrored themselves to their own eyes by a constant register of their daily experience; observing their actions with conscientious fidelity, anatomizing their feelings and motives to the very life tissues of their spiritual being, and noting down the whole with scrupulous exactness, as if to have before them, for correction or encouragement, just as either may be required, the changing features, with their still more changing expression, of that "hidden man of the heart," which to every one is, in fact, the only true man. But whatever these fail to detect, they bring much into view which must otherwise be concealed; much for others to inspect as well as for themselves to profit by. They admit us to their deepest privacy, open to us the inner chambers of their souls. They make us familiar with thoughts which they would hardly whisper but in solitude, and companions of a history which unfolds itself secretly, under the sole eye of Omniscience. They may not intend this, and in many instances do not; if they did, the motive would often condemn the performance. But while intending only their own good, or, intending nothing directly, but just talking to themselves in writing—soliloquizing with the pen, as some men get into the habit of soliloquizing in speech—they bequeath to us a legacy of most peculiar preciousness. For there is hardly any one, certainly no one of eminent gifts or services, of whom the portraiture thus self-executed—and all the more faithfully because unconsciously—would not charm by its vital interest, or improve by its practical lessons.

It were greatly to be wished that something of this kind existed of Mr. Ridgway. He was several times importuned to prepare at least a few notes of his laborious and not uneventful career; but, though half consenting, he never really set himself to the task. There is hence but little known of his private life—the life I mean that is lived apart from all outward observation; the life that thinks, feels, acts, and no one knows it; the life that weeps, prays, rejoices, struggles, wrestles, triumphs, and no one sees it. Such a life Mr. Ridgway had, as we shall learn from one or two momentary glimpses which he himself has given us, though for the most part his life was rather public than private. All was exposed, and all was expressed. Long retirement would have been irksome, a painful repression of powers that could not readily be turned inward upon themselves, or only for the collecting of new resources to be employed in some practical way without. Still a few touches of self-portraiture are given by him in a diary of a visit made to America in the year 1822. This diary extends over a period of about four months, each day having its separate record, and is interesting, not only for the variety and fulness of its details, particularly as referring to American scenery, institutions, &c., but as presenting a very suggestive picture of his general character and life. All is wonderfully methodical in arrangement and minute in statement, even to the least important business transactions. Moreover, all subjects occupying his attention are brought together, each one in its place—commerce, politics, education, religion, home, his class, the church; so that nothing stands out from the rest, but things are told in their order, just as they occurred, and just as he saw and felt at the time, giving us the warp and woof of his every-day life, without confusion of their threads, or any attempt at other pattern than the one which they naturally took; while religion, in some pious expression or devout prayer for himself and others, ever comes in at the close, as if to wind up and sanctify the whole. Mr. Scott, who knew him so well, and to whom I am indebted for this diary, as for much else that I am not likely to forget, says of it: "This diary is very characteristic of Mr. Ridgway, and is as much like the last twenty years of his life as of any former period. There is the same energy in business, the same restless activity, the same sentiment of religion pervading everything, the same love of domestic pleasures, and the same longing for Bethesda and his religious associations. There is also the power of observation, and of recalling and describing what he has seen and heard, which we have so often seen displayed. Indeed, upon the whole, I regard it as an interesting *souvenir* of the portion of his life to which it refers, and a proof of the persistency of his feelings and habits, which, like his handwriting, are the same, and his own."

Much of the diary is given to business; a considerable portion of it to American hospitals, prisons, educational establishments, churches, &c., and is now out of date, though worthy to be quoted in a few extracts, if only to illustrate Mr. Ridgway's habit of observation, and the kind of things that attracted his special interest: only a small part of it is of a character most to be desired for the purposes of this memoir. It extends to nearly 300 pages of manuscript, and thus commences: "September 9th, 1822. Left my dear friends and home for Liverpool, and reached there safely in the evening." This, be it remembered, was some years before travelling was "made easy" by steam, and when a visit to America was a rare and almost adventurous achievement. Mr. Ridgway was probably not a "good sailor;" he was certainly not exempt from the ordinary penalties of those who "tempt the deep," as the following entries will show:—

"Sept. 15th, Sabbath-day.—Still sick, but on deck. Found opportunity to read and meditate; distributed some tracts to the sailors, and was glad to observe their general good conduct and conversation. Many thoughts of Bethesda and privileges at home; an humble trust in God, and a gracious sense of His presence and favour."

"Monday, 16th.—A strong but favourable wind, high sea, and ship pitching greatly; very sick, and all day on deck. . . Read the blessed Bible, and Raffles' 'Lectures' on deck. Had to complain of much insensibility and coldness of heart. Thought of my class, and waited in prayer with them. Felt much for my beloved wife and afflicted sister." On the next day is this memorandum: "Read a work on ecclesiastical establishments of Europe, and a plan for regulating that of Great Britain—equal in cost to them all. This, decidedly my best day, spent a large share of it in reading and meditation, and not forgetful of home." Again: "Thought too much of home and my concerns. Endeavoured to cast all my care on Him who careth for His people."

"Sunday, 22nd.—Many sweet reflections this day, and the sacred volume very profitable. Thought of my beloved wife and family, of Bethesda, and the blessings of a Gospel ministry. Entered into the spirit of David's feelings: 'How amiable are Thy tabernacles, O Lord of hosts! My soul longeth, yea, even fainteth for the courts of the Lord,' &c. &c." On the following day: "Examined my papers; considered my approaching duties; read a little profitably, and then met my class in spirit, although 1,200 miles absent in body." Again: "Finished Raffles' 'Lectures' to-day. Made 1,500 miles and upwards. Completed Savings Bank Rules, &c.; began a series of useful minutes, with a view to treasure them to good purpose. Read my Bible with pleasure, and wish to value it more and more." Once more: "Commenced Wardlaw's 'Sermons on the Socinian Controversy,' and much pleased with them. This is a very favourable day with mind and body. Felt a pleasing anticipation of the approaching Sabbath, and could have wished, yet dared not wish, I had been permitted to spend it elsewhere, and in other company."

"Sunday, 29th.—The third Sabbath on board the ship. . . . Opened the day with meditation and prayer; continued with reading the Scriptures and Wardlaw's 'Sermons;' enjoyed many profitable reflections in the consideration of present and past mercies, reminding me that David's language, Psalm ciii., should properly be mine. I feel the want of David's grateful and devout spirit, and pray that it may kindle and ever burn within my heart. Felt a pleasing union with my Christian friends at home, and earnest breathings for their spiritual welfare. . . Was gratified to see increasing attention on board the ship; gave some tracts out; passed the evening comfortably." Again : " Read two or three chapters before breakfast ; worked at Rules of Connexion a couple of hours afterwards ; read Wardlaw in the afternoon for about the same time ; enjoyed the evening variously. So far the voyage has been highly prosperous ; two-thirds done in less than twenty days. God be praised for His goodness, and oh, my soul, be thankful."

"Sunday, Oct. 6th.—Arose early. A delightful morning, and nearly a perfect calm. The sky cloudless ; the sea a sheet of azure, sparkling in the rays of the sun, which were like a path of burnished gold. Viewed the scene with delight, and a portion of David's feeling, ' How wondrous are Thy works, O Lord,' &c. Took my Bible, and cultivated this feeling until breakfast hour ; afterwards joined my family in spirit, and accompanied them to the house of God, with devout wishes on behalf of them, and all assembled there. Entered upon Wardlaw's second volume, and felt my religious opinions confirmed. Accompanied the captain in his boat, to try the current, which ran one mile per hour to the south-east. The ship looked majestic on the water, but nearly motionless. . . . Observations taken, &c. ; we had made $60\frac{1}{2}$ degrees, but to-day no progress, for the ship drifted north instead of west. Closed the day with reading, meditation, and prayer, and felt an humble sense of the Divine presence." On the day following we read: "Commenced a new version of Mr. Wesley's hymns, in order to combine employment with utility.* A month from home to-day; how glad should I be to know its occurrences; but I will trust in the Lord, and not be afraid. Every blessing attend thee, Sophia, and friends, and my class. Grace and peace be with you, and all Israel. Prosecuted the perusal of Wardlaw, and of the Holy Scriptures, and at the close of the day was enabled to add, 'In the multitude of my thoughts within me, Thy comforts, O God, delight my soul.'" Similar jottings continue throughout the whole voyage. Each day are found such as the following: "Worked at Wesley's hymns a couple of hours." "Rose refreshed and strengthened. Prayer and reflection seasonable. The Scriptures sweet, and the example of the Redeemer truly worthy of imitation." "To-day finished Wardlaw's second volume: a valuable work, and highly satisfactory to the lover of the truth as it is in Jesus." "Thus days get on, whether improved or not. Turned to my Bible, and read with pleasure of the love of God in Christ Jesus my

* By "a new version" is doubtless meant a new compilation. This compilation was afterwards succeeded by another, while just now a larger and much better one is in course of preparation.

Lord. During this twenty-four hours we have made but little progress. Great need of patience, and how wise to cultivate it, since in disappointment it administers both consolation and hope."

"A month from Liverpool to-day. Long in passing, but short now past. Thank God for sparing, and for daily mercies. This has been a sort of new month in my life, and so long as I live shall I reflect upon it with gratitude."

"Sunday, Oct. 13th.—Entered upon this precious day in a devotional spirit. I felt it to be the Lord's, and though disappointed of a seat in His earthly house, I worshipped under the canopy of heaven. The day, as every Sabbath day has been, was remarkably fine. I read and meditated on deck, and soon the heavenly fire kindled; in spirit I united my praise and adoration with friends at home, and found the force of Mr. Wesley's sentiments—

> 'What though our bodies part,
> To different climes repair,
> United still in heart,
> The friends of Jesus are.'"

The next day finds him again at work on Mr. Wesley's hymns; the "evening" brings his "flock to remembrance," and closes with the Doxology: "Blessed God, thanks for Thy goodness. O, my soul, praise the Lord." Tuesday witnesses the completion of "the first or rough draft of Wesley's hymns," at the close of which "a joyful voice" is heard from the mast-head, "Land, ho!" "A fine view" is obtained of "the promised land" on Wednesday morning, and ere the night sets in the "desired haven" is gained, with this for a final acknowledgment of Divine mercy throughout the thirty-three days spent at sea: "Again, thank God for His goodness, and O, my soul, devote thyself to Him."

From this time Mr. Ridgway's diary includes all his business transactions, together with observations on whatever he sees and hears (and he contrives to see and hear much), besides a record of his thoughts and feelings in their graver and strictly religious moods; all woven together in a continuous narrative of each day's occurrences. Much of what he describes is doubtless different now from what it was forty years ago, and much more, it may be, was, because of the rapidity of his view, imperfectly apprehended at the time; but the extracts given will serve to illustrate his power of observation, as well as the class of objects which attracted his notice. Here is a description of the capital of New England. "Took a promenade through Boston. The town is finely situated at the west of the Atlantic, with a fine open bay, and large, secure harbour, the entrance to which is fortified by two forts, enfilading each other. The approach to Boston is enchanting, and especially in the spring, during which the little fairy islands in the bay are clothed with verdure and gaiety. Across the harbour, which is capable of containing several hundred vessels of the largest burden, stands the town of Boston, the appearance of which is highly imposing. No docks are to be found here, as in Liverpool; all round the town, to the harbour, are quays or wharves, where the vessels lie in perfect safety, owing to the harbour being so finely protected from the north-east winds. The Central, India, and Long wharves are remarkably fine and convenient, with rows of buildings opposite kept by the merchants, &c., in which the goods are directly stored from the ships; these buildings are exceedingly lofty and valuable. . . Mercantile speculation and shipping are the *forte* of this place, and few seaports, I apprehend, exceed it in boldness and extent of speculation, or in the excellency of the ships. The town is surrounded by the sea, save on one side, on the south, where a neck or isthmus of land connects it with the country. After passing the navy yard, say from Charleston causeway to the said isthmus, it is navigable only for small craft, but the flux and reflux of the tide, together with the constant presence of salt water, give several advantages together—salubrious air, fine view, and the means of wealth. Across these waters are fine causeways, one of stone, the rest of wood, with gates, tide gates, &c., the whole of great length, and constructed at great cost, leading into the country in various directions: on all these roads are tolls for foot and horse passengers, and at each crossing or re-crossing you pay. Although the general effect of being thus surrounded with sea water is healthy, yet I suspect it occasions a serious degree of humidity in the atmosphere, and renders the night air dangerous. The streets of Boston, at least of the old town, are narrow, and the houses constructed without much taste or regularity, partly of bricks (remarkably small), but chiefly of wood. In the centre of the town are several fine streets; in the upper or new part streets of handsome houses rise from the sea to a fine eminence, at the top of which stands the State-house, commanding delightful views, and offering most healthy, and either cheerful or retired, situations to their owners. In the best parts of the town the streets are built of brick, with a few principal ones of white granite, obtained from a distance of thirty miles, and worked in the state prison. As the old houses are taken down, handsome streets, &c., replace them, and the city of Boston will soon rise to a noble uniformity of street architecture. Land is very valuable, as high as five or six dollars a foot in best situations, and every eligible site is eagerly bought up. I observed a strong disposition in mercantile men to vest money in buildings, especially on retiring from business. In some parts of the town, particularly in the west or rising part of it, are a great number of houses absolutely princely in their appearance, not a few of them built in good taste, combining comfort with elegance. Many are built of red brick, well faced and well laid; others of granite, and others again of wood, covered with slate, or shingle painted to imitate slate; but even the wood houses, being painted, look well, and add a pleasing variety to the general appearance of the place. These houses and streets abound with small gardens and shrubbery wood, forming, except in the connected building of the streets, a series of country-houses. At the south of the town is the Mall and Common, being the only promenade and open ground in the place. The Mall, or rather ground of which the Mall is made, is a gift for that purpose, subject to forfeiture if perverted from it. The Common is Corporation property, laid down in turf, of a triangular shape, enclosed with railing, with a pond in it, good walks, &c., and is used for the troops to parade in, and for general Hyde Park purposes on high and fine days. The trees in the Mall are indifferent, and past their meridian: in the Common are a few young trees, but not promising. On the west, or State-house side, is a fine range of houses, commanding a delightful view of the Mall, Common, sea, and opposite hills. On the north and east also are handsome rows of houses. St. Paul's church stands at the east, a large Calvinistic Independent church at the south corner. Upon the whole, this is the finest part of Boston both in situation and respectability. With these remarks I will close the observations of the day, and, indeed, of the week. I have abundant cause, on reflection, for gratitude and devotion. This has been a week of mercy; the Lord is good, and blessed be His name. O that my beloved wife and friends may experience the same goodness, and join me in ascribing thanksgiving and praise to Him who sitteth on the throne, and to the Lamb."

His first Sabbath in the New World is thus given: "Sunday, Oct. 20th.—I am rejoiced to see a return of the Christian Sabbath, and to be privileged to spend it in a manner suitable to its institution. It is the sixth Sabbath since I left my home, and the seventh since I was permitted to tread the courts of Jehovah's sanctuary. O Lord, said I, and with Christian sincerity, I have loved the habitation of Thy house, and the place where Thine honour dwelleth. My morning's services of prayer, devotion, and reading the Scriptures were profitable, and I felt peculiar pleasure in commending my wife and Bethesda friends to the Divine blessing. After breakfast, I walked to Mr. Wilby's, intending to spend the day in the bosom of his family. In the morning we attended Divine service at St. Paul's: the minister, Dr. Jarvis, of the episcopal order; the service after the manner of the Church of England, only adapted to the peculiarity of the country, the President and people of the United States taking the place of the king, &c., in the collect for that purpose. Dr. Jarvis is a judicious divine, and his discourse, though not very energetical nor learned, or deeply doctrinal, was nevertheless impressive and useful. The congregation was more respectable than numerous; the place a model of neatness, after the style of the Parthenon, with a plain colonnade in front. The ceiling is coved, and in sunk compartments; the altar a beautiful circular recess, with Corinthian pillars; the pulpit handsome, and the pews well constructed and commodious. This church cost upwards of £20,000 sterling, and is calculated to seat 1,200 persons; is supported at great expense by an assessment on the pews, which are private property; the minister has 2,500 dollars per annum, and the organist 450 dollars. This is a specimen of American episcopal establishments of modern date. After dinner we attended the Independent or Congregational chapel, a spacious place of worship, and well filled with about 1,200 hearers. The regular pastor was absent, and we were informed a student from Cambridge Academy was appointed to officiate. The minister was young, and of humble talent; the audience respectable and attentive. In Boston few of the churches have services in the evening; I therefore accompanied my friend to a rehearsal of sacred music, the choir, both instrumental and vocal, all of Boston. I was both surprised and gratified with the place, the assembly, the orchestra, and the performance. I was delighted to see Handel honoured in America as he is in England, and to hear his solos, duets, and choruses given with a taste and execution rarely surpassed in any place with the same population. The whole performance, arrangement, and conduct were highly becoming, and though I felt and expressed myself opposed to such things on the Sabbath evening, yet I could not regret enjoying a treat which it was not likely I should soon have again. . . . . . From hence I returned to my hotel, revolving the enjoyments of the day, thankful for the same precious gospel in America as in England, pleased with the similarity of language and worship, and praying that God may bless and prosper His Word in Boston, according to the riches of His grace. Afterwards I looked a little into my Bible," &c.

The week succeeding this first Sabbath in Boston is given partly to private business, but more, apparently, to objects of public interest, especially to such as would be likely to attract the sympathies of a man of large philanthropic affections. His immediate design in going to America was to push the trade of his firm; but, while this was no doubt attended to with a diligence that left nothing practicable undone, schools, news-rooms, athenæums, halls, infirmaries, jails, houses of recovery, lunatic asylums, &c., were inspected and described, as though to see and report upon them was the only object of his leaving home. "In humble dependence on the Divine blessing," he goes to his agent, and "endeavours to forward his concerns there;" repairs to the Town Hall (Faneuil's Hall) "held in high veneration by the Bostonians, and containing a fine full-length portrait of General Washington," the veneration arising from the fact that there, or in the old hall which this has displaced, the citizens "met, and determined on asserting their independence;" takes an artist round the city, to "select the best objects for sketching to be applied to a set of American scenery," that is, to grace the pottery of Cauldon Place; finds his way to the book shops, where books are found "to be exceedingly dear," and thence to every place which a man of large human sympathies, and of energy which hardly any labour could exhaust, would be likely to visit. Two extracts must serve as specimens of many entries and minute descriptive details.

"In the course of the morning I visited the English classical school, conducted by Mr. Emerson, and was exceedingly gratified with the result. The system of education in Boston is begun early. In each of the twelve wards are three or more primary schools, or, as we call them, dame schools, where children are allowed to remain up to seven years old. In these elementary schools about 2,500 are taught. From hence they are removed to the public schools, of which there is one in most wards, conducted by a master and usher, and containing each from two to three hundred scholars. These schools contain 2,200 children, duly separated; and in them are taught reading, writing, grammar, and arithmetic; but the scholars are too numerous for the masters, and these schools are capable of great improvement. At ten years of age, those boys who are qualified, and whose parents wish it, are removed to the English classical school before named, where they are perfected in the previous branches, and instructed in geography, history, natural history, belles lettres, poetry, &c. &c., by the system of question and answer, with explanations, &c., whereby the children are taught to think, understand, and retain the subjects of instruction. The discipline of the school I found excellent: the boys all alive by emulation to rise above each other. 'Blair's Universal Preceptor' and 'Tytler's Ancient History,' with 'Walker's Dictionary,' and many of our best school-books, I found in use. This school is a neat brick building, three stories high; the lowest story is one school, of the amphitheatre form, the second and third are divided, but all the boys seated in rows one above another. The master has a fine command of the boys, and they with their desks before them have every convenience for books, &c. From this school boys duly qualified, and whose parents wish it, are removed at thirteen years of age to the Latin school, conducted by Mr. Gould and assistants. This school is in high repute, and is constantly full, and is confined to the children of the Bostonians. Besides the classics, are taught mathematics, navigation, and the higher departments of knowledge. The leading merchants, &c., received their education at this place, and their children are following their example. Indeed, the last two institutions provide so excellent a system of education, that other schools—I mean boarding-schools—are little, if at all, wanted. One thing is remarkable, viz., that education is provided by the state, or rather by the town at large, an annual tax being imposed for its maintenance. Schools are ordered where and when wanted; a committee of education is appointed, consisting of one or more in each ward; these associate to themselves others, so arranging matters that all the schools are visited at least weekly, and a report made every year. Parents have therefore only to find their children books and clothes, and few remain uneducated. The children of the rich and poor are indiscriminately taught together; the only distinction is ability. The children of the poor rarely go to the upper schools, because their parents want their services; on the other hand, the children of the rich cannot rise to them, unless by their proficiency they become qualified. Little opportunity for Lancasterian schools here, and only a limited field for Sabbath schools. Certainly I am pleased with the Boston system of education; it will rear intelligent characters, and fit for the respectable situations in life. Yet it wants extending to the poorest and to the coloured part of youth; it may be said, 'there is still room;' but if the state of education at Boston be a fair specimen of what prevails throughout the United States, it is undoubtedly beyond my expectation."

The minuteness of this account is explained by the practical interest which Mr. Ridgway always took in popular education, having himself originated various schemes for its promotion, and personally spent large sums of money upon it. The notes were probably made for future use, to be applied in some serviceable way to the advancement of an object so dear to him in his own neighbourhood; while the admiration manifestly conceived for the system of scholastic training pursued in Boston, including its means of support and general results, was that probably which afterwards inclined him, if not to a scheme of local taxation like that adopted in the State of Massachusetts, yet to an appropriation of public money, in some form of equitable distribution, towards the furtherance of popular education in this country.

A second extract: "After attending to the special business for which I came here, I accompanied the chaplain of the State's Gaol in a visit to it. This gaol is situated in the west of Charleston, across the water, and is approached by a causeway bridge guarded by a toll-gate, at which all passengers, whether on horseback or on foot, pay every time they pass it. My guide I found a worthy, pious man, and employed in doing good. We were admitted without ceremony into the gaol-yard, and introduced to the governor, who ordered a keeper to attend us. The gaol is of rude stone, dark granite, and surrounded with a fir palisading of great height. It consists of a centre for the governor's and warders' use, and two long connected wings for the prisoners' sleeping-rooms and cells; the whole very clean and well ventilated, but the rooms too small for the number of beds in them, and a bad plan of suspending one bed over another. A distinct ward is set apart for an hospital, another for a place of solitary confinement—the latter, as I was told, rarely used; yet this is the only means of punishing the refractory. In the front of the gaol—that is, the north-west front—is a scene of bustle and activity such as is rarely seen in a place of confinement. Fifty persons at least are employed in squaring, tooling, and chiselling granite stone, brought by canal and coastwise from the country, as far as thirty miles off. Here stones of all descriptions, for walls, pillars, cornices, &c., are worked both for public and private use; and I was told a large order was going to be shipped for New Orleans. The institution is national; and as there are no stone-yards but this in the town or near it, and as the consumption is great, it must prove a means both of public ornament and public benefit. I observed, in addition to this, a manufactory for brushes, bearing the London and Liverpool marks; another for cabinet goods; a third for weaving; besides shoemaking, tailoring, picking oakum, &c. &c. Work is found for all, according to their strength and ability; if weak, a physician fixes their quantum, and, after performing their task, all are allowed to make some spare earnings, which are given them when released. No females are confined here; they are kept in the town gaols. No persons are sent here until after conviction. Little classification seems to prevail—indeed, it seems hardly possible by day, although it might be after the hours of labour; but the more serious prisoners, if such there are,

are allowed to retire and pray together for a short time during each day, and the chaplain converses with them without interruption. A chapel is appended to the gaol, and the prisoners attend divine service in the morning and afternoon. I found about 350 persons in this unhappy place; some of them of hardened appearance, while others turned aside from observation. A few only were ironed, none were chained to each other, or prevented from locomotion. I observed the prisoners wore pantaloons, each leg of a different colour. The governor of the State has power to pardon, except in cases of punishment ordered by the General States. The town prison of Boston is old, small, mean, inconvenient, and filthy. The want of arrangement and of every comfort was so thoroughly felt, that a new prison is now erecting on the banks of the water opposite to Charleston; and, judging from its present appearance, will be spacious and complete, capable of the best arrangement, and favoured with a fine sea breeze for its constant ventilation."

After an inspection of many other places, of which something is said of each, the Sabbath gives our traveller rest and spiritual enjoyment. "Sunday, Oct. 27th," he writes, " I rose improved in health and spirits, for which I thank God. I employed myself in prayer, meditation, and reading the Word of God, carrying my thoughts and affections to my home, Bethesda, and the scenes present in imagination, although distant in locality. My feelings were well employed, and I almost regretted the summons to breakfast at eight o'clock." Three public services are attended this day, a marriage witnessed, and a funeral; all of which are set forth in detail. The service in the afternoon, which was to have been conducted by "the most popular orator in Boston," was presided over by one who seems to have been a celebrity in his way. In personal appearance he is described as a curiosity, even where, since persons are found there from all quarters of the globe, curiosities are not rare. A species somewhat lower than man is specified as the type which he most resembles, and a costume far otherwise than what would be called ministerial as that which best characterizes his dress. His oratory seems to have been as curious as his appearance, and the substance of his discourse in keeping. It was "not, indeed, without some quaint and even striking remark;" but was "inconsistent, unintelligible, raving, and extravagant in the general." He was "a weak vessel," and one at least of his hearers was sorry that he "should be allowed to sound before so large a congregation." He was very "energetic and vehement," yet, says this sorrowing hearer, "I heard no loud responses, nor saw any popular effervescence. Either Mr. D. was too flat, or the people were too flat, or the combustible matter does not prevail here so extensively as my information described it." Something else was observed here, nor here alone: "A prevailing habit in almost every one of turning his head round to look who comes in, and of looking about the congregation, until the minister enters the pulpit;" and, further, "a most indecorous haste in getting out of the place, scarcely allowing time for the benediction." Something much better than this, though it might have been better still: "A couple of upper galleries filled with coloured people (black), very decently dressed, and deeply attentive," with the closing reflection, "The poor have the Gospel preached unto them." The evening service was in a Baptist chapel, and the sermon preached by a Yorkshireman, "from the testimony of God concerning Cornelius," Acts x. 4. "It was a very telling, judicious, and seasonable discourse," says our visitor; adding of Dr. B., the regular minister of the congregation, who finished the service, "a fine, plain old gentleman; I observed him, in appearance more of the good Mr. Bull, farmer, than like a D.D.;" and winding up with the observation: "Here, as at the Methodist chapel, I had the pleasure to contribute my mite to Missions, but I observed that the boxes were much larger than the hearts of the people to fill them." The day is brought to a close thus: "I was glad this day to terminate its duties; yet it had been a day of enjoyment, especially the morning and evening; but on my return home, I allowed myself to engage in worldly conversation; the proper affections of the day had been chilled, and I had to recollect how needful it is not only to hear, but to watch over and cultivate, the Word of Life. I retired to rest not quite so comfortable in mind as usual, but humbled under a sense of the Divine goodness, and blessing God both for me and mine."

In bidding adieu to Boston, on his return to England, after a tour embracing many of the chief cities of the Northern States, Mr. Ridgway says: "Before leaving Boston, I ought to say that I was exceedingly pleased with the liberal and spirited character of the place. In trade the merchants are industrious and enterprising; in habits, friendly and hospitable; in manners, at first reserved, but if cordially met, free and agreeable; in religion, unfortunately too loose and superficial, preferring their own notions and selfish feelings to an humble obedience to the Son of God. This is the darkest trait in the picture of the upper classes of Boston, and hence Unitarianism has obtained a popularity which threatens the most painful consequences. Happily, however, there are many even in Boston who hold fast the true faith; and after the cheerless night of error shall have passed away, I trust the true light will shine with greater and wider lustre. I attribute the influence of Unitarianism at Boston to the prevalence of worldly and pleasurable motives and feelings, and I believe the same effects will generally result from the same cause. In the middle circles at Boston a much better religious feeling prevails; and in few places have I seen a more ample provision of churches and chapels, a better attendance on divine worship, or a more respectful observance of the Lord's day. The working classes are in comfortable circumstances, and make in society a better appearance than the same classes do in England. I saw few, indeed, who were very poor, and not a single beggar in the streets. The aged, infirm, and orphan find a ready reception in the workhouse; while every man able to labour obtains employment and competence. So far as my observation went, I saw little drunkenness either in private or public, yet I was told that this dreadful evil was very much on the increase; and certainly this is to be feared, since from the cheapness of spirituous liquors, a man may get intoxicated for sixpence. Against this danger, the interests of morality, industry, public order, and social happiness are all engaged; and I do hope it may never spoil the fair character of the Bostonians. The political character of the citizens is said to be 'Federal,' but, in the general, it appears to have become republican; indeed, the only difference I could observe was, that one party wished for an aristocratical preponderancy, a second for a pure democracy. Danger probably would attach to the ascendency of either influence; a third or middle party has therefore to spring up, which shall act independently, and turn the scale, not in the direction of party, but in that of constitutional principles. 'Federalism' is no longer the watchword for monarchical government, but simply for the landed and mercantile interest: the people at large are jealous of the name as well as of the principle, and it is easy to see that it will gradually weaken and wear away."

These latter selections are made from Mr. Ridgway's journal, not as being the best, but as being for the most part continuous, and as referring to objects having some local connexion with each other, though comprising much less than the whole of what he has written respecting them. Nor are they made for any particular merit they can be supposed to have for the general reader, though forty years ago, when America was virtually much farther off and much more rarely visited, their interest would probably be greater than now; but they are given for the few incidental glances they afford into that more retired part of Mr. Ridgway's life, which must else have been closed to our view. Other similar selections, embracing the same variety of topics, might be made, extending to several chapters; but it will be sufficient for our purpose to add to these just concluded a few passages taken almost at random.

Here is one. It is Monday evening, October 28th, 1822. In the morning, at two o'clock, Mr. Ridgway starts by coach from Boston to Albany. This is among his preparations for the journey, and not the least important, assuredly not the least profitable: " O Thou in whose hands are the issues of life and death, keep Thy servant in all his ways. Prosper his journey; support him in health and strength, and crown him and his beloved wife with Thy grace and favour. . . It is seven weeks since I left my friends and home; seven weeks of peculiar mercies. May it be my happiness yet to go on and prosper, improving these mercies to the best of purposes, and rendering to the Giver an undivided heart. My class, to-night you meet; and I meet you in wishes for your spiritual welfare. May you do well, and all your prayers be heard and answered."

In a few days we find Mr. Ridgway in "the celebrated town" of Philadelphia, having taken a tolerable inventory of the objects which lay in his route: passing through more than one "sweet little village;" enjoying a sail "150 miles down the river Hudson, with great pleasure indeed;" catching a view of New York, of which the "situation is perhaps one of the finest in the world," but a visit to which is, for the present, postponed; pleased with the scenery here, regretting that the land is not turned to better account there; ascertaining the means of education in this place, and the accommodation for Christian worshippers in that; in danger of falling into temptation one moment, but victorious, by the grace of God, the next. Disappointment meets him on his arrival, and great loss, owing to the bad management and "thorough shipwreck" of an agent in whom confidence had been placed. "The tale was as bad a one as could be told." "For a while I was depressed," he testifies, "but I endeavoured to cast my care on the right Object, and to look up." Moreover, the next day was "the day of the Lord," and this brought with it composure and rest. "I arose early," he says, "and strove after a spiritual frame of mind. The Word of God was sweet, and the morning prayer refreshing." Public service is attended in a Presbyterian church, of beautiful classic design and great finish. From 1 John v. 19, a "learned" discourse is heard, but possibly not "fitted to do much real good," at least to those who are hungry for "the sincere milk of the Word." The congregation respectable, but no prayer for a blessing on entrance, none at departure, but haste to get away; so that "while the blessing is pronounced, the people put on their coats and hats, and off with them before it is well-nigh finished." Another service is attended—Baptist this time, the congregation being large, but "indecorous and unaccommodating;" while of the minister it is noted, "he has a beautiful voice and engaging address: of all the men I ever heard he read a hymn the best, and I never listened to one who so much excelled in his petition for peculiar cases and persons." The day comes to a close with thoughts on what has been heard, and thanks for the privileges of the house of prayer.

As in Boston, the prison is visited, and is found "unlike what you would have expected to see in the far-famed prison of Philadelphia. It is ill-contrived, ill-managed, ill-looked after, with bad—nay, cruel arrangements; no instruction, no advantages. Four hundred men and forty women occupy this dreary abode, enlightened by no teacher or teaching, for the task of benevolent endeavour has ceased, and no Howard or Reynolds enters here." The description is extended and painful, but we leave it for another one. " From the prison we went to the Hospital, a fine building, with two handsome wings, and spacious grounds and garden. The centre building contains two wards, of eighteen each, for men, and the same for women; no other ventilation than through them, and the cooking places at each end of the wards. There is a ward for fever cases at the left, and a range of rooms for lunatics. These pay from three to fifteen dollars a week. Many also of the patients pay, and a small subscription completes the means of annual expenditure. I obtained a yearly statement—yet, strange to say, there is no code of laws. There is a good library, physician, and medical rooms at the entrance, and an operating room underneath the observatory. The building does not seem to be made the most of; a great deal of room is lost. Six doctors attend in rotation; but, so far as I could see, the thing wants the inspection of vigilant benevolence. The public here are too much alive to getting money, and these public institutions are neglected.

In front of the institution is a fine statue of William Penn, in bronze, on a marble base. He it was who gave the valuable and spacious ground on which the hospital is erected. . . . We then went to the workhouse, or, as it is here called, 'Bettering House.' This we found an immense establishment, with upwards of 1,200 inmates—the most pitiable, afflicted, helpless, and deplorable creatures my eyes ever beheld. The mixture of black and white, the ill-clothed and dirty, the pale-faced and wrinkled, the infirm and aged—oh! this was a scene that harrowed up humanity. Here was a picture of wretchedness exceeding, I will venture to say, anything of the kind in England. No beggars are allowed in the streets, and it is well, for the beggars here are beyond description. Where so many blacks are, not slaves, there will be a great deal of poverty; but at least the best should be made of the case. A proper classification is wanting, proper cleanliness, due ventilation, &c. But the children, I was told, are instructed; a doctor attends the sick, and divine service is performed on the Sabbath day. I obtained a copy of the rules and report of the accounts, and shall be glad to find the system better than it appeared to be. The governor and matron are appointed by the citizens; the expense is borne by assessment, after the manner of our poor-rates; and this, I was informed, was very high. Persons are rarely refused admittance, but the work done is trifling. The whole system requires inspection."

I have chosen this extract rather than any other, of which there is abundant selection—one describing the "Academy of Fine Arts, an humble imitation of ours;" another "the banks of Philadelphia, splendid buildings, more like temples than banks," &c.—because it illustrates the habitually philanthropic temper of Mr. Ridgway's mind, and presents the gratifying spectacle of a manufacturer, yet pushing his fortunes, visiting a distant country mainly for the purpose of trade, turning almost daily aside from this, that he may look upon poverty, sickness, crime undergoing punishment—extremest wretchedness of nearly every kind—for the sole end of gratifying a benevolent desire in witnessing the provision made by a young and thriving nation, lately come into possession of whole centuries of Old World experience, for the support of the destitute, the succour of the afflicted, and the reformation of the erring and the outcast. The like spirit in all our Christian merchants, or in any considerable number of them, manifested in the thousand possible ways of self-forgetting humanity, would redeem our commerce from the reproach of vanity and selfishness now only too justly brought upon it, and convert it into a ministry of grace and goodwill, of which all classes, directly or indirectly, would share the benefit.

In Washington a similar round of visits is paid, and notes taken accordingly. The city is described, its situation, the architecture of some of its chief buildings, its one street stretching "from the capitol to the President's house, a mile and a half long at least, and forty yards broad, or thereabouts, besides footpaths and rows of poplars, the whole laid out in three divisions." The capitol and Houses of Congress are pronounced "splendid buildings," and their splendour is brought out in detail, not omitting the splendour of the cost, "five millions of dollars, and not yet finished." "The building is in imitation of the Roman capitol, and certainly does credit to the taste and spirit of the nation." Two pictures are seen in "this colossus of a building," of which, or rather of the two great historical events which they memorialize, the Americans are doubtless proud, and with reason; one of them representing the Declaration of Independence, the other the surrender of Lord Cornwallis's army.

Again, the like thing is repeated at Baltimore, on his return, with the addition of a

Sunday's experience there. This Sunday differs in some particulars from preceding ones; perhaps from having no one to guide him, as in other places. He attends the cathedral, and is surprised to find himself in a Catholic place of worship; hears what he does not understand, and sees what he cannot think will profit. He goes to the Unitarian chapel—this time, as it would seem, consciously and deliberately. "Found it, as described, a very handsome building." Justifies this opinion by a full length portrait of it, calling it, in the final touches, "very attractive," "the temple of ease" to "a fashionable audience." The sermon, however, was to him less "attractive" than the building; "it was dry, the service formal, and the whole a mere apology for religion or religious worship." In the evening the benefit derived was not much greater, though the service was strictly evangelical. But then this service was long, "especially the sermon, more long than interesting." "Two hours and a half" were consumed in the whole, making it nine o'clock ere the hotel was reached. This was certainly "long" enough for penance, but too much for profit. "But"—and here chagrin gives way to charity, with a faint streak of humour in it—"the minister was a Scotchman and a stranger, and that circumstance must be his apology." The day was lost, in the sense of positive enjoyment, though it commenced with an "endeavour to forget the world, and to sit with Christ in heavenly places," and ended in "retirement, for meditation and repose."

Of Baltimore a more exhaustive survey was taken than of some other towns, with the customary visits to Gaol, Penitentiary, Poor House, &c.; observing of the public buildings that the "people were proud of them, and not without cause," though wondering at the paucity of country seats round the city, and that said people should "prefer the convenient streets to the open and more healthful fields." But to avoid repetition, or at least additions of similar things, we omit the descriptive catalogue of our traveller, and accompany him homeward in "the mail coach, which has nothing—as to comfort, or company, or speed—to recommend it but its name." Nor stop we on the journey, though he stops more than once, and offers some inducement to us to do the same, until we meet him, "glad to be so far back on his way to Old England," in New York. Great labour attends him here, and much of a like kind has been gone through, making "rest acceptable," before he arrives. Some discouragement also meets him, making his "mind hurried and wandering."

Moreover, there are no tidings from home, which is the more trying, because he left a beloved sister there ill; and desires, with a deep and tender anxiety, that she may be spared. "I expected letters," he writes sadly, "but, alas! I was disappointed. Singular to say, I have received but one letter from home during my stay in this country. I trust it prognosticates no evil, yet I cannot help indulging some fear. Merciful God, if it seem good in Thy sight, avert from my house the day of tribulation, and spare Thy servants to praise Thee. I will not give way to alarm, but rather trust in the Lord." But now it is the Sabbath day, and his is the wonderful power of dismissing the past, and of giving himself wholly up to the present. The anxieties of the week therefore are not allowed to disturb the repose, or to interfere with the spiritual occupations, of the day. "Oh, blessed Sabbath," he had said the night before, "what should we be but for thy return! I shall enjoy it—the rest, the meditation; and will now prepare for its duties and blessings. May God help me and my Sophia!" And so the Sabbath comes, and this is part of the memorandum made upon it:—

"Sunday, Nov. 24th.—Awoke with the satisfaction of knowing that this was a day of rest—rest from earthly labour—and of spiritual employment. I commenced its duties with reading and prayer, by which my better feelings were profited. I scrupled not to let my thoughts run across the Atlantic to my beloved wife, and relatives, and Christian friends, who have the first, the warmest affection; the others my best wishes, especially in the religious engagements of this day. After the bustle of a public breakfast (calculated to make you long for the comfort of a private, or say domestic one), I walked round the town a little, both on the north and east sides... I went to Mr. B.'s chapel, and for once heard a Universalist sermon, from 'Diligent in business,' &c.; but by no means to my satisfaction. A pleasing, but dangerous doctrine this, the extreme even of the liberal Arminianism. Afterwards walked and dined with Mr. and Mrs. D., at whose pressing entreaty I remained during the whole of the day, talking over old affairs, of friends in England, &c., the Church of God, &c., until I found it near nine o'clock. Repaired to my quarters, displeased with myself for not having made a better improvement of this day, and determined to be so unfaithful no more. Early I retired to my chamber, to humble confession and prayer. I felt comforted and blessed beyond my deserts."

The following extract contrasts strangely with

what we know of American feeling in this year of grace 1862.

"Monday, Nov. 25th.—This was the day of the evacuation of Boston by the British troops. It was kept therefore as a holiday, or rather as a day of commemoration. The troops paraded, feasts and entertainments were given, flags were flaunting, and bells ringing; but all passed off quietly, and without any unpleasant effervescence of feeling. Indeed, so far as I have been able to remark, the animosities of American feeling have greatly subsided, and are fast extinguishing ; and are likely, especially if the pulpit and press promote this end, to die out, from want of fuel." Alas! the press is much more rancorous in its spirit now than it was in 1822, and is too much —at least too selfishly—interested in blowing the fire, to withhold any fuel it may have to give.

A few lines on the Empire City, taken from most copious memoranda, must bring these notes of travel in the Western World to a conclusion ; and these are given, I again repeat, not as possessing any value apart from the little power they may have of illustrating some features in Mr. Ridgway's character.

"New York is situated in latitude 40° 2' N., in longitude 74° 1' W., and is built on the south-west end of the Isle of Manhattan, now called New

York. At present the city extends from two to three miles in length, and is of unequal breadth. It contains a population of 120,000, having increased with great rapidity, and likely to increase with still greater. Never was a place more favourably situated for commerce than New York. It is near the ocean, yet protected by the Narrows on one side, by the Sound and the pass, Hell Gate, on the other. By means of the Hudson river it has the finest communication with the north and west—a communication now nearly extended to the lakes by means of canals; to the east it is open by the Sound, and by the numerous rivers which empty into it; and to the south-west by the sea and the Rariton river, to which is to be added a canal across to the Delamere. Vessels of any burden come up to its wharves, and lie there in perfect safety. The Sound or bay is protected both by nature and by art, and few spots present a greater combination of beauties. On one side is the Isle of Staten, on another, Long Island, on a third the coast of Jersey, on a fourth the little islands of the Sound. On all sides you are charmed by scenes of luxuriance and loveliness—especially must this be so in spring and summer. Entering New York, you are struck as much with its noble appearance as its fine situation. Debark at the Battery Point, before you is the fine street of

Broadway, running from Point right through the town to the country. Parallel to this are other similar but inferior streets, one of them to the left called Greenwich-street, leading to the village of that name, where the inhabitants retired during the late fever. . . . The New York houses are principally erected of brick, kept neat and clean by being painted; the bricks and mortar lines looking always new, without being gaudy. A few houses are of stone, and the number is increasing; here and there is a splendid house of marble. The open places for promenades and recreation are the park (already described), the Battery Walk by the sea-side, the Bowling Green, and the Bowery." Then follows a complete inventory of the principal institutions. "The places of worship in New York are numerous and respectable; the congregations are large, the ministers, I believe, of moderate talents, and they and the people liberal and friendly. . . . New York appears to shine in its charitable institutions for widows, orphans, seamen, &c. No beggars are found in the streets. Here is work for the industrious, provision for the sick and aged, and a penitentiary for the lazy and disorderly. Here are also a great number of social institutions of a literary, friendly, and political nature, such as are sure to keep alive the spirit and energy of the place. The city has a mayor and corporation, but the citizens retain all power in their hands, and of this power they appear most jealous. . . Men in office seem to court popularity more than duty. . . . Education appears to receive a growing attention both from the city authorities and the people. Several schools are established on the Lancasterian plan, and others are in contemplation, as well as some of a classical kind. These will gradually supply the present obvious deficiencies, and place the youth of New York on a level with those of other parts of the State. An Exchange and Public Hall are much wanted here. Indeed, notwithstanding the splendour of some of the buildings, and other features of great interest, there is room for many improvements, and improvements are much needed; and considering the wealth and spirit of the place, it is only fair to presume they will ere long be made. . . The commercial enterprise of New York is truly surprising. To see the shipping lying all round the town, the imports and exports, the warehouses and wharves, the busy shop and bustling street, is really a marvel. By this means, and this only, can you form an idea of the business of New York. She is a sort of emporium to all nations. Her commerce is to and from all parts of the world. *Their* merchants often find the capital, *hers* enjoy the profit. The markets are abundant, and the prices reasonable; rent and education high; taxes about 10 per cent. on property; advantages and privileges great; and, were I to live elsewhere than in England, I think it should be in New York."

Notwithstanding the frankness of this last remark, and, indeed, the admiration it implies of the city he had just slightly sketched, the necessity would have been very great that would have fixed Mr. Ridgway's residence anywhere but in the England he loved so well; and though few were more inclined to give or repay a compliment than he, I suspect his strong national predilections would, in like circumstances, have hurried him into a similar breach of good manners to that committed by his countryman, who, when a pleasant-tempered visiter from the other side of the Channel observed to him, that if he were not a Frenchman he should like to be an Englishman, replied, with more honesty than politeness, that if he were not an Englishman he should wish that he were one. But now his heart yearned towards England with a special fondness, though mainly because there was the little charmed circle within which his domestic affections palpitated with life and glowed into rapture, and the yet larger circle, next in his tender regards, over which his religious sympathies expanded with a more than human charity and a higher than earthly joy. Long had seemed his absence, and often had he chastised his impatience to return; never, however, doubting that God would at the right time conduct him to the home that was so precious and to the friends he loved so much. And now the prospect of this was very near, and looked very bright. His heart bounded at the sight of it, and he gave himself up to its rapture. "Can it be doubted," he had inquired a short season before, when leaving Boston for the second time, and taking the first decisive step homewards, "can it be doubted that I was in excellent spirits, and that the morning, though snowy, was to me a delightful one? The fact is, I was bound for home; and so long as I hastened forward, nothing could be unfavourable."* What then must be his joy now? For this was his last day as an exile, at least his

---

* "Si vous interrogez des Anglais voguant sur un vaisseau à l'extremité du monde," says Madame de Stael, in her *Corinne*, "et que vous leur demandiez ou ils vont, ils vous repondront: *home* (chez nous), si c'est en Angleterre qu'ils retournez." Perhaps it required a foreigner, accustomed to a different type of domestic life from our own, to speak of an Englishman's attachment to home as something observable and peculiar. Unhappy would it be for England as a nation, as well as for Englishmen as men, were this attachment to lessen. It is this which gives such truth to the grand saying of one of our foremost living orators—"The nation, sir, the nation is in the cottage."

last day on land; and every future step must bear him nearer, not only in time, but in actual distance, to that magnetic centre towards which his heart had so long turned, and vibrated with such tremulous emotion. Moreover, this last day was the Sabbath, to him "the pearl of days;" and specially welcome in this instance, as giving him quiet preparation for the voyage just at hand, as well as repose from labours just completed. Accordingly we find him, early on the morning of December 8th, in this jubilant yet prayerful mood: "I awoke with immediate recollections of my approaching departure. Soon I was packed and prepared; yet before I left my chamber I paid my humble tribute to that gracious Power which had surrounded me with His protection, and brought my pilgrimage in the Western World to a close. To the same Power I commended myself while crossing the great deep, confident of this, that in His hands I should be secure from harm. I turned my thoughts to my beloved Sophia and my friends; and though the Atlantic was between us, yet with my face towards them I felt cheered and happy." In a few hours more, having spoken his kindly adieus to a number of friends who had gathered round him at parting, and taken security of his memory for the execution of certain friendly commissions in England by noting them down in his Journal, he was looking back with admiration on the fading outlines of New York, and forward—though with another organ of vision—to "home, sweet home."

Each day of the voyage was occupied very much as before, when his course was in the opposite direction; and as similar entries recur, the extracts need be but few.

"Sunday, Dec. 15th.—Thank God for the light of another Sabbath morning, of a day of instituted rest. I arose with the feelings of those sweet lines—

'Welcome, sweet day of rest,' &c.

In these feelings I knew my beloved wife would participate; and I sincerely pray that the first Sabbath of the new year may be spent with her under the influence of these feelings, and with hearts of overflowing gratitude to the Father of all our mercies. This morning I spent in reading, devotion, and meditation. Ah! how did I long for the courts of the Lord's house, for the temple of the living God. And if I longed for Bethesda above all, surely this was but natural. Peace be within thy walls, thou favoured of the Lord, and prosperity within thy palaces! And may peace and prosperity attend all the churches of our God throughout the world. I was glad to find my fellow-passengers impressed with a suitable sense of the sanctity of the Sabbath day. Several Bibles were produced and read during the day. In the evening we sang a few hymns of praise, in which some six or seven joined, and at an early hour retired to rest."

"Wednesday, Dec. 25th.—On this day it was my purpose to be in England, but Providence has otherwise ordered it. Certainly never did I more exert myself to accomplish an object, and I feel I ought rather to be thankful in having done so much than to regret not having done more. After breakfast I took my Bible, and read of the nativity of Christ. The subject was delightful; and the benefits of Christ's advent came home in a real experience. I felt, I trust, a measure of love to Him who loved me, and gave Himself for me. Aid me, O Lord my God, to renewed acts of devotion, and to one continued consecration to Thee. In the ship we had some useful conversation on the events of this memorable day; and I was glad to find that our Bibles were in requisition, showing as it did that the advent of the Saviour, though too little valued, was not forgotten. I read a sermon with considerable pleasure, and, thinking of the labours of Mrs. Hoffman, the mistress of the New York Widow and Orphan Institution, determined on recommending my beloved wife to copy her example in doing something for the relief of unfortunate sufferers of that kind.

. . "On retiring below, my mind was led to reflect on the closing Sabbath of 1822, on the end of the Sabbath, on the privileges and ordinances of this year—all gone, or well-nigh gone, into eternity, carrying to the Book of the Divine Remembrance my misimprovements, neglects, and unfaithfulness. Oh, how little have I learned this year under the preaching of God's Word; and by what I have learned how little have I profited! How many Christian privileges have I had in the courts of the Lord's house; but how few of them have I turned to profitable account. How many seasons for reading, meditation, and prayer has my gracious God placed in my hands; but how frequently have I omitted these duties, or with lifeless feelings engaged in them. In the church, in my family, in my closet—yea, in my heart—much has been wanting; and most heartily do I now crave for mercy and forgiveness through the prevailing merits of my Redeemer, purposing through His grace and the help of His Holy Spirit to lead a new life to His glory, to redeem the time, and especially to improve His blessed Sabbaths. I do love the Sabbaths of the Lord; and henceforth I, and my wife, and my house will endeavour to keep them holy, labouring on these blessed days more anxiously for the bread of life than we do on others for the comforts or riches of this perishing world, that when our earthly Sabbaths shall come to a close, it may be our happiness to enter upon a Sabbath that shall never end... With these feelings I turned to my Bible, closing the day with devout prayer, and so retiring to rest, saying with the Psalmist, 'Thou, O God, art still with me.'"

Several days are consumed in successive calm and storm, during which no progress whatever is made. The calm is such that the vessel refuses to answer her helm; the storm is so sudden and so violent, that fears are entertained for her safety. Delay is the least evil; yet even delay, when the danger is past, is felt to be a heavy disappointment. But the rising impatience is at once checked by the reflection: "Our times and seasons are in His hands who knows what is best for His servants, and to His appointments I desire cheerfully to submit.

> 'Good when He gives, supremely good;
> Nor less when He denies;
> E'en crosses from His sovereign hand,
> Are blessings in disguise.'"

The last day of the year has the following record for memorial: "I desire to close the year under a devout impression of the unbounded goodness of

God towards one of the most unworthy and unprofitable of His servants. On board the *Robert Fulton* packet I raise my Ebenezer, and declare 'Hitherto hath the Lord helped me:' helped me in difficulties, preserved me in dangers, strengthened me in weakness, established me in grace, and led me in the paths of righteousness for His name's sake. Unto the Lord belong praise and thanksgiving; but unto me shame and confusion of face, so ungratefully have I requited Divine favours, so partially—or, I ought to have said, so slightly—have I improved them; so small my attainments, so slow my progress, so earthly my pursuits; and so imperfect, not to say sinful, my best performances, that I am only astonished at the favour and long-suffering of God. 'His mercy endureth for ever.' Oh, may His tender mercies, and my unbounded obligation to Him—increased as both have been during the past year, and especially during this distant voyage—deeply affect my heart, and lead me under the influence of His grace to more inward holiness, and more entire devotedness of life to Him. Oh, that health and strength, time and talents, body and spirit, with all the gifts and blessings entrusted to my stewardship, may be henceforth improved to the end of their bestowment—the glory of God, and the furtherance of my present and eternal salvation. It ought, it must, it shall be so this ensuing year, as thou, my Father and God, shalt help me. To thee I commend myself and my beloved wife, praying that the year 1823 may be our best and happiest. To thee I commend all our concerns, imploring thy smile and benediction upon them. To thee I commend dear relatives and friends, praying that health and happiness may attend them. And to thee I commend thy church and people, earnestly supplicating that prosperity and increase may be their portion throughout the world. And now I shall peruse the Word of God with a well-tuned heart. I will retire to rest at peace with God and man; my meditation shall be sweet; and when I awake to-morrow, I trust I shall be nearer heaven and nearer home. Even so. Amen."

While omitting much else, the closing entry— because it is the closing one, and highly characteristic and fitting as the close—must not be omitted.

"Saturday, the 4th January.—I arose this morning as though I was awaking from a dream, and found the whole a welcome reality. Instead of a narrow berth, I was in an ample bed; instead of a rolling ship, I was on steady land; instead of the Atlantic, I was in Liverpool; and in a few hours I should be on my way home. Alas! in the absence of letters, again fears and anxieties arose for the health and welfare of my affectionate wife, and for the life of my afflicted sister. Still I dare not but trust God, I dare not despond. At an early hour I took breakfast, then called on ——, made several little purchases, and after clearing out at the hotel, threw myself in the 'Aurora' coach—and, though the day was gloomy and the weather wet, yet I thought it the most pleasant ride of my life. Many, and sweet, and profitable were my cogitations; but soon after ten o'clock I arrived at Newcastle, and my thoughts gave way to feelings still more delightful. My gig was in attendance; by eleven o'clock I was at Cauldon Place, and in a few minutes in the embraces of my beloved wife. Thanks and praise to God, I found her perfectly well; my sister still declining—but gradually, and without much suffering; all other friends well, and doing well. I received their congratulations with heartfelt joy; appeared the next day with devout thanksgiving in the house of the Lord; and now conclude this Journal with a solemn resolution, by Divine help, to be, more than ever and for ever, fully the Lord's. Let it please thee, O God, to make me and my Sophia thine on earth and in heaven. Amen. Amen."

CHAPTER VII.

Politics and Philanthropy.

CHAPTER VII.

POLITICS AND PHILANTHROPY.

Two qualities are prominently exhibited in the foregoing extracts from Mr. Ridgway's Journal, his piety and his philanthropy. Other qualities come into view, but these specially, and with abundant illustration. The piety is not conventional, nor is it sectarian. It is not attachment to a particular denomination, or to particular forms of service, that is expressed, but something deeper and diviner. It is a love to Christian institutions and to Christian truth and worship; a delight in the Sabbath and the sanctuary, such as only true godliness can know; a fellowship of spirit, arising from a secret kinship of regenerated nature, with those of like precious faith with himself, producing a feeling of loneliness, isolation, and almost exile when absent from their society in the customary means of grace; a chastened humility of soul, which bows before God in sorrowful confession of sin, but rises from His feet rejoicingly, in full assurance of His recovered smile; a profound and prevailing sense of His ever-watchful and all-encircling providence, such as finds in each daily deliverance and each recurring enjoyment a new proof of His care, and looks to Him, with the simplicity of a childlike faith, and also with the confidence of a well-assured experience, as to one who is ever present to hear, and ever waiting to help.

There are all the marks of genuineness and truth in this portraiture of Mr. Ridgway's inner life. The picture is not only executed by himself, but executed unconsciously; certainly with no view to its exhibition, or to any use of it apart from his own immediate profit. He did not know that he was sketching his own character; he knew only what he thought and felt, and he wrote down what he thought and felt, just as he wrote down the sights he saw at sea and the business he did on land. His thoughts and feelings are of the true Christian stamp. They have all the characteristics of a simple and beautiful piety. Beautiful such piety always is, wherever seen, for there is meekness in it, humility, reverence, childlike simplicity, self-abnegation, and self-surrender to God through Christ; but most beautiful does it appear when seen in one who has wealth and worldly influence, whose position gives him authority, and whose powers invest him with command.

Mr. Ridgway's philanthropy was as real as his piety, nor less active. It was partly the growth of his piety, though founded originally on a strong natural instinct of humanity. He was essentially tender, and was easily moved by the presence of suffering. No one could be sterner, when conviction or duty required sternness; but few would melt sooner, where penitence pleaded for forgiveness, or want appealed for help. Tears were ever answered by tears, and sorrow rarely told its tale without unsealing a kindred sorrow in his heart. The sight of even an imaginary grief had power to touch him to the quick. A beautiful illustration of this is communicated by the Rev. John Taylor. In the Great International Exhibition of the present year is a picture by Ansdell, called "The Lost Shepherd." It represents a Highland shepherd lost in the snow. Death is unmistakably on every feature and in every limb. The shepherd's dog is there, but it also is dead, the severity of the storm having been sufficient to kill both. The dog lies on the dead body of its master, having gone there to warm him into life again, or perchance to lessen its sense of utter loneliness by feeling that he is still there; or it may be, after its last wail of distress, led by an instinct that is almost human, that it might be undivided from him in death as it had been in life. The shepherd's wife, following the search of another dog, kindred to the now lifeless one, has just found her lost husband. Her elbow is on one knee, her face in her hand, weeping. At a little distance is the living dog, weeping too, in its way. With raised head and dilated nostrils, from which the steaming breath is made visible by the biting cold, it is sending up a cry of wild and helpless grief, hardly less affecting than the silent and motionless sorrow of the brokenhearted widow close by. The scene is in the mountains, where nature, sterile at the best, is now under the absolute dominion of a rigorous winter.* This picture belongs to John Whittaker, Esq., of Hurst, and was painted for him by the artist. Mr. Ridgway, in one of his visits to Hurst, not very long before his death, sauntered into his friend's gallery to relieve him for a time for the discharge of some pressing business. The picture was a new and large one, and readily took his attention. It was a touching one, and soon wrought upon his sympathies. He stood before it transfixed, unable to control the emotion which the sight awakened. In the meantime Mr. Taylor entered, not knowing that any one was there, and was surprised to see the strong man " with face

---

* Death reigns supreme over all, with only so much suffering life in the midst as to make the sense of his unpitying and resistless empire the more complete and painful.

quite swollen, and the tears rolling fast down his cheeks." Startled by the sound of footsteps, Mr. Ridgway turned quickly round, aroused from his reverie, and with quivering lip said, "Oh, I am so glad nobody's in distress but myself; it's only a picture."

If a philanthropist is one who can say, "I am a man, and nothing that is human is alien to me,"* then does the honour of this character belong to our departed friend. But if a philanthropist is one whose life says this rather than his speech—who, while loving his kind, does not exhaust his love in mere talk, or but partial giving and working in favour of distant objects and speculative schemes, but does the thing that is next to him first, as the duty that is most urgent, and looks in the face, with a benevolent purpose to relieve it, the want or the woe that he encounters in the everyday walks of life, not waiting for opportunities of kindly service, but making more opportunities than he finds—as Lord Bacon says a wise man will do—then was Mr. Ridgway a philanthropist after the truest and best type. There is a philanthropy, more ideal than practical, which expends itself in projects for wholesale dealing with human ills, and pays but little regard to individual cases of privation and suffering that exist immediately under its eye. So there is a benevolence, if such

* "Homo sum, et nil humani a me alienum puto."—*Terence.*

a name may be given to it, which, as if under the anodyne of selfishness or sheer indifference, seems for the most part to sleep, but wakes up now and then at some fortunate juncture, or in answer to some pressing appeal, and wins a life-long reputation by single gifts which are large enough for every one to know, and every one to speak about.

Mr. Ridgway's philanthropy was practical and particular. He was benevolent from nature, but he was also this from principle. In him sentiment was pervaded by conscience, or rather regulated by it; so that what was a gratification of feeling was at the same time an obligation of duty. In all public movements designed to give relief to the suffering or redress to the injured, he took an active part, giving as he had ability, and working with his might. He threw himself ardently into the cause of Negro emancipation; laboured long and much for the removal of civil disabilities from those not connected with the Established Church; became an advocate of peace, though not, as it is now the fashion to stigmatize all such advocacy, "peace at any price;" strove in many ways and by various measures to improve the condition of the poor, and thus to lessen the amount of pauperism and crime. His efforts for these last objects had mainly a local reference, and they were connected with many other similar efforts having a like reference. A writer, in a journal not likely to be too much biased in his favour, having, in a well-written article on his character, just after his death, contrasted the past and present of the pottery district, continues, in allusion to Mr. Ridgway's share in the change: "Only by this contrast can we realize the idea of how much there was needed in the way of public improvement when Mr. Ridgway first entered on public life. And let it here be understood, that we do not arrogate for him the merit of all that has been accomplished. His public exertions were, of course, principally made on behalf of his own town; but in various ways his influence extended throughout the district. While still a young man he saw what was needed, and he set himself to promote it with an amount of goodwill that recoiled from no difficulties, would own no defeat, and rarely failed of success. In some things he was a pioneer, in others he entered the field later; mostly he was a leader, though not unfrequently he accepted a subordinate part; but on whatever he undertook he left the impress of his own strong will, and was felt and acknowledged to be a power of himself. . . Although differing from some of his views, we must still describe him as a man of sterling principle and genuine philanthropy. The abolition of Negro slavery, and the removal of civil disabilities from Dissenters and Roman Catholics, afforded him heartfelt gratification, which he could not have found in any exclusively party triumph. He was also a social reformer, long before social science associations were heard of. The better administration of the poor-laws engaged much of his attention. He combated dauntlessly, year after year, the abuses of the old system in the populous parish of Stoke-upon-Trent, and himself devised a scheme which would have combined most of the advantages of the new poor-law, without altogether depriving the guardians of discretionary power, either over their own officers, or as to the mode of administering relief. He was an ardent supporter of popular education," &c.

During the prevalence of the Asiatic cholera, while many were spell-bound with fear, he was in every place where action was needed, and in every service in which help could avail. Now he was driving ministers of religion to the dying and the dead, again he was sending relief to such as were smitten but might recover, and often might be seen visiting the miserable abodes of the poor and the profligate, to get them whitewashed and cleansed, in order to save their inmates, as well as their neighbours, from the ravages of the disease. At particular seasons, and especially during winter, his bounty lighted up many an humble dwelling, and made many a widow's heart sing for joy. In not a few instances, "when the ear heard him, then it blessed him; and when the eye saw him, it gave witness to him: because he delivered the poor that cried, and him that had none to help him." But often the benefactor was not known, because the benefit was indirectly conveyed. He had almoners of his bounty, who executed his commissions under instructions of secrecy. An aged minister informed me that his wife was one of these, and another lady whom he knew a second; that munificent were the charities which these at different times dispensed, and yet that the author of them was never known but to themselves and their husbands. Those who, from whatever motive, spoke harshly of him, were not, when in need, excepted from his generous regards; for, as the writer before referred to says, "many a detractor has discovered that his was the kind, though unknown hand, that helped him in distress." He had regular pensioners on his purse, and a small number of these continue to enjoy his bounty still, though he himself has now resigned his stewardship. His gifts, in fact, were incessant, and mostly so given as to enhance their value. They were seldom very great, and this was sometimes mentioned to his discredit by those who for a particular object desired a larger contribution. But then he was never rich, according to the modern standard of riches. Few have had such opportunities of becoming so as he. A colossal fortune was, humanly speaking, easily within his reach; but then to reach it he must give less, or at least, must himself be and do less. Do less for others by doing more, as men speak of doing, for himself. He must give to his own business much of the attention that was reserved for other objects, and be known rather as a successful manufacturer than as a social reformer or a public philanthropist. Moreover, if he seldom startled by a large donation, he could always be depended upon for the support of any worthy cause, giving ever without grudging; and, in fact, ever giving. His benevolence was not a solitary shower, sudden and violent, interrupting a long season of drought, as some men are surprised into a generous deed once or twice during a whole life of habitual stinginess; nor a mountain flood, which comes only after an abundance of rain, as some men give only under the joyous excitement of a fortunate speculation, or after a long period of unwonted prosperity; but a continuous stream, flowing on with a tolerable uniformity of depth and current—now in the open plain, and again under friendly shade of drooping tree or mossy marge, but ever pursuing its determined course, and becoming broader and deeper towards the end. And *at* the end; for of what remained of his property when he died, several thousand pounds were bequeathed to objects which were first in his benevolent solicitudes during life.

The descent from philanthropy to politics is not very great. Nor is there any descent at all, if both be rightly understood. The principle in both is the same, and the spirit is the same, where the philanthropy is real, and where politics are not degraded into a profession, or pursued from personal ambition or for worldly interest. The professional spirit dishonours every pursuit. It is the spirit of pride or selfishness; and out of these passions nothing that is good can come, except by that mystery of Divine operation which educes good out of evil. This is too commonly the spirit of political parties, causing them to degenerate into hostile factions. Rarely is a high-minded philanthropy the motive to political life or to political measures; while yet no grander field for the exercise of such philanthropy can be chosen than that which political life presents. Patriotism itself is only philanthropy intensified by its restriction to one's own country; but how often do politics derive their inspiration from patriotism? Seldom, it is to be feared, but in great national crises. Doubtless there are certain tendencies in our minds which answer to the conventional meaning of the terms conservative and liberal, or fixed and progressive, and in few cases do these tendencies respectively correct and balance each other. So there are certain divisions in society, with interests seemingly peculiar to each, which operate to foster one rather than the other of these tendencies, while each naturally gives rise to a distinctive political faith, and, in constitutional states, generates a party and a policy for its support and furtherance. The faith may be honestly held in both cases, and in both may be animated by a philanthropy equally sincere; and where this is so, little else than substantial good will spring even from their emulations and collisions. But, unhappily, the faith often exists only in name, and the philanthropy hardly in pretence. Accident or interest too frequently determines the party chosen, and a temper of sheer exclusiveness or intolerance suggests the measure to be promoted. When the parties meet in open competition, it is mainly for a trial of their relative strength. Real principle is apt to disappear in a mere desire of party pre-eminence and power. A vehement spirit of rivalry is kindled, in the fire of which, for a time, all noble sympathies and charities are consumed; and, as on the field of battle, whatever will weaken or wound the enemy is resorted to, and even justified, as legitimate warfare.

It is this which so often makes, and always tends to make it injurious for Christian men, particularly men of influential standing in a Christian church, to occupy a leading place in the local struggles of political parties. No one has a better right than they. No one should have a higher qualification. No one perhaps has so great an interest in the questions involved, since their interest is not only civil but religious. Still, there is more than temptation in the course; there is nearly always something of positive evil. The arena is one in which the conflict must be, as things now are, both sharp and bitter. Few can enter it without being blinded and choked now and then in the dust and heat raised by the violent commotion and the rude encounter; without at times both grieving friends and embittering opponents; without occasionally doing that which a calm judgment must condemn, and a generous heart is sure to mourn over. The individual himself suffers, suffers in that which piety holds most dear; and through him, by at least the enemies of Christianity, " the way of truth is evil spoken of."

Mr. Ridgway did not escape this necessity, as, not only was he a politician, but an active and ardent one. He could not be lukewarm in any cause which seized strongly on his convictions, much less therefore in that which addresses, as few things else do, the principles we esteem most highly, or the prejudices we cherish most blindly. "Within the borough of Stoke-upon-Trent," says the local authority, whose testimony we have more than once cited, "Mr. Ridgway was for many years the acknowledged leader of the Liberal party, and promoted successively, with a characteristic ardour which occasionally brought him into unpleasant collision with his opponents, the return of Mr. Wedgwood, Mr. Heathcote, Colonel Hanson, and Mr. Ricardo, the latter of whom has continued to represent the borough for nearly the last twenty years."* The honour he thus did so much to confer upon others, was several times urged upon himself, but he wisely judged that his sphere of usefulness lay elsewhere than in the House of Commons. His "lead" of the Liberal party was by no means confined to parliamentary elections, though, as the borough was hotly contested, and the more difficult to contest because it embraced several towns, each of which had a predominant influence of its own, it was then that his lead was most availing, as it was most conspicuous. But, in fact, it extended to all

* Since this was written, Mr. Ricardo has been removed by death, and another now occupies his place.

occasions in which a lead was required, and to every question which broadly distinguished the Liberal party from the party opposed.

His qualification to lead was gained in the great struggle that closed with the passing of the Reform Bill. In this struggle he was deeply concerned, uniting with some of the foremost, as also some of the best, men of the county to promote it. The struggle is now but little remembered. A whole generation has passed away since it occurred. The lapse of years has dimmed the recollection of it to many still living, who witnessed its stirring scenes, and felt its palpitating excitement. Other events of great national interest have succeeded, in fact have been consequent upon it, which, because more recent, have displaced it in our thought. But no event within the present century has transpired of equal importance with the passing of the Reform Bill. None have had an influence so widespread and so multiform. Other measures have operated directly and in some specific way, but this indirectly and universally, rather as a new force that could be popularly applied to national interests in general, than as a single provision affecting one interest in particular. This it was, doubtless, which to the aristocracy of the day made it an object of such relentless hostility. No measure of modern times was ever opposed with such determined resistance, and in face of such alarming threats and dangers; and none was ever pressed with greater ability or with a nobler courage. A few at first represented the feeling of the many, but soon the many represented themselves. The question was not confined to the Houses of Parliament, nor to professed politicians. The people became a parliament, in perpetual session, for its discussion. The whole nation threw itself into the contest, and kindled to a heat that bordered on revolution. Though a question in which the middle and trading classes were most interested, yet the classes next to them made it their own, and clamoured for it as if the benefit would be wholly theirs. Disappointment only nerved, and defeat almost exasperated them. Exasperation best describes their spirit at more than one juncture. In the great centres of manufacturing industry, the people, headed not by irresponsible adventurers, but by the wisest and wealthiest of the citizens, flocked together like electric clouds, and swayed under the excitement of the hour like a forest shaken by the tempest. If they were resolute, their opponents were obstinate. If on their side were signs of rebellion, on the other side were threats of armed repression: while yet it was doubtful, or not doubtful, just perhaps as men wished it, whether the army, if called upon, would act at all. The moment was critical, and each day became more critical, especially as everything tended to this result, and in the end came to this result—that King, Commons, and People, for the most part, were opposed to the House of Peers, and the House of Peers, by repeated majorities, was opposed to them. It was hardly a question which must ultimately yield; happily there is little occasion now, from any disappointment with the measure, to remember which *did* yield.

Of the many speeches which Mr. Ridgway gave at this juncture, a few passages from one may be here extracted, not of course for their present importance, but as illustrating his general style of address. It was delivered at a county meeting, during the great excitement occasioned by the defeat of the Reform Bill in the House of Lords. Mr. Ridgway seems to have discussed the whole question. His address is divided systematically into several particulars, which he considers in their order. He starts with the statement, that the question of Reform is not a modern one, that it has grown with the intelligence of the people, that it is the fruit of painful experience, and is now so urgent that it cannot longer be postponed. He then defines the kind of

Reform that is wanted, and the mode in which it is to be effected; relates what has been done to obtain it, and tells the result thereof. " And what will the people now do?" he goes on to ask. His answer is: "They will not be fickle, nor silent, nor sulky, nor outrageous. They are not Frenchmen, but Englishmen. The cause is not one of pet or passion; it is one of principle, rooted in their judgments, their affections, their hearts. Delay makes it more valuable; experience makes it more indispensable, and opposition makes them more determined and immovable. . . It is the cause of their king and their country; it is the cause of liberty and good government; it is the cause of public peace and public well-being; it is the cause of agriculture and of commerce; it is the cause of all ranks and classes, even of the hostile Lords, since whatever exalts and benefits and unites the nation, must exalt and benefit them too. . . . What then will the people do? They will be patient, but firm; they will be orderly, but unanimous; they will hope, but they will not rest in hope. They will keep alive the flame of liberty. They will rally together, and will rally round their friends. Action, and not reaction, will be the order of the day. The voice not only of thousands, but of millions, will be heard; their late repulse will animate their courage and inflame their zeal. Union will make them immovable, and energy will make them irresistible. And as our intrepid soldiery at Waterloo rushed onward to the charge and snatched the victory from their enemies, so will the nation collect its forces for the coming conflict, and make the field its own. The crisis is eventful, and most earnestly do I hope that the Peers will be wise, while they have it in their power, to listen to the voice and obey the will of the nation. But, gentlemen, let the worst come to the worst, the Peers of England will never be permitted to dictate and control the King, and his faithful Commons, and his loyal people.

"Mr. Sheriff, we seek no interference with the Peers. We envy not their honours, nor covet we their wealth. We assail not their privileges, much less encroach upon their rights. But if they are so blind to passing events, so ignorant of public feeling, so little acquainted with the increased wealth, but above all the increased intelligence of the nation—if through jealousy, or prejudice, or self-interest, they continue to oppose the united voice of King, Ministers, Commons, and twenty millions of the people — assuredly they will have cause to tremble for the consequences. Hitherto, the people have been patient, because they have rested in hope; but as hope deferred maketh the heart sick, hope extinguished may make the nation furious. The Peers of England may be mighty, but it will be seen that they are not almighty. . . But, say the Lords, we are not opposed to Reform, but only to the Bill. O yes, ye doctors, one has this nostrum, another a second, another a third. One likes this part, another hates that, and a third pleads delay; but all agree to reject the Bill, because the people demand it. Not even a committee can be granted. The people ask for bread, and they give them a stone; they petition for their rights, and are reviled, first for their patience, then their impatience, now for their ignorance, and again their unreasonableness. There is no pleasing these Lords, but by throwing out the Bill, and granting the people nothing.

"And why should the people be so intent on this Reform Bill? Because they have long and severely felt the want of it. They trace the want to years of misrule in the carrying on of sanguine wars, in the lavish expenditure of the public money, in the creating of an artificial state of prosperity of which the natural effect was the greatest adversity. They see and feel it in a national debt of such enormous size, and in hosts of sinecures and pensions. They see and feel it in many a statute of wrong and injustice. They see its necessity in the Corn Laws, in the existence of slavery, and in numerous monopolies. Yes, gentlemen, the public see and feel its necessity. They are bent upon carrying it. They cannot be diverted from their object; and the longer it is delayed, the more urgent and extensive will be their demands.

"A reform will tranquillize the nation. It will remove the cruel and arbitrary distinctions which have too long prevailed. It will bring men of business into Parliament, who will do their work better, and with sympathies more in accord with the people. The Peers will maintain their privileges, and their honours too, so far at least as they deserve them. An arrest will be laid upon corrupt government, and a course of legislation adopted that will develop and improve the resources of the country, and promote the well-being and happiness of all classes.

"Mr. Sheriff, with such a cause, with so much unanimity, with so much patriotism, we will neither fear nor despair. Our good king is still on our side, and I pray God to preserve him for the sake of his people. Earl Grey, my Lord Brougham, and their excellent coadjutors are still at the helm. Though not the modern, yet the ancient nobility of England are still with us. The Commons are faithful, and the people are firm. The enemy shall not dare to insult us about reaction. They shall not have to triumph in our silence. Nor shall they drive us to desperation. No, no! We will not tarnish our weapons. We will not dishonour our cause, nor grieve our king, nor embarrass his ministers, nor discourage our friends, nor injure our enemies; but this we will do,—we will assert our rights as Englishmen; we will demand them constitutionally, and so as that there shall be no reasonable pretext for withholding them. We will be united as the heart of one man. The ministers will know their friends; the king will exercise his royal prerogative in the creation of as many liberal-minded Peers as, concurring in the national sentiment, will be able to give effect to the people's wishes. The hand of Providence will bring us two blessings instead of one: we shall have a reformed House of Peers, emulating the noble deeds of the Commons. The Reform Bill will be passed triumphantly; the grievances of the people will be gradually redressed; Great Britain, restored to quiet and prosperity, will again lift up her head, and present to the admiring world the picture of a regenerated and happy people."

This address is in the excited spirit of the day. It is hardly a reflex, because in fact too tame for this, of the intense feeling that was let loose by the defeat of the nation's hopes in the obstinate resistance of the House of Peers. It would hence be wrong to infer from it any leaning towards democracy. Indeed, it contains evidence of a very different leaning. It is not of the existence of the Upper House that Mr. Ridgway complains; he rather singles out the *ancient* peerage for honourable mention; it is of the unreasonable opposition manifested by it to the will of the other estates of the realm, and to the wish of the people generally. "He was not," so witnesses the authority before adduced, "a man of extreme views, led away by violent counsels, or prone to change. . . In truth he disliked demagogism. His counsel to many young persons who sought his advice in that troublous time was given in the spirit of the wise man's words—'My son, fear God and honour the king, and meddle not with them who are given to change.'" His loyalty was not merely a felt obligation, but a rooted sentiment, almost a passion. It cropped out in his speeches almost incessantly. There was something in it of feudal reverence and courtly ostentation. Especially was this so with reference to her present Majesty. Nor only because of her universally acknowledged virtues, but also because of her sex. He had a most chivalrous regard for woman. In him the spirit of ancient gallantry seemed to live again. His politeness was almost excessive, yet never obtrusive. There was a complimentary ease and grace of manner, with a pleasant humour, shining through a delicacy of sentiment and fluent propriety of speech, which ever made it a pleasure to a lady to receive his attentions. This regard for the sex greatly intensified his feeling of loyalty to the reigning sovereign, and gave to his frequent allusions to her a touch of even affectionate homage.

I remember a characteristic illustration of this. For many years in succession, he was chairman of an annual tea meeting held in connexion with the Conference of the body to which he belonged. This meeting is always a large one, no room, scarcely, in any town, being too capacious to hold it. It is also for the most part unusually interesting and exciting; first, because of the large number of ministers and influential laymen present, and secondly, as being an attractive centre and occasion for the exchange of yearly congratulations, to friends united in the same connexional fellowship, from nearly every part of the country. It was Mr. Ridgway's custom, in taking the chair, to glance at some of the most important events of the year, whether civil or ecclesiastical. Seldom was this done without a loyal and cordial reference to the Queen. At the meeting which took place after the Great Exhibition at Paris, the customary review was taken, and the customary allusion to her Majesty was made; but in this case, in more than usual detail, and certainly with much visible feeling. Towards the close of his remarks he said, "I was in Paris, at the Exhibition, during the time her Majesty was there, and I was rejoiced at the enthusiasm which her presence everywhere created. I had often seen her in her own country, and witnessed with pride and pleasure her bearing towards her people, and the people's bearing towards her; but in Paris Frenchmen vied with Englishmen in doing her honour, and she was equally gracious to all. I remember on one occasion, when her Majesty was passing along the Rue Rivoli, I advanced a step to make a respectful bow to her, and a French official checking the attempt, I turned upon him and said, 'That is *my Queen*, sir!'"

What strikes one again and again in connexion with his public life, in fact in connexion with his whole life, is Mr. Ridgway's immense capacity for work. He delighted in doing, and hence was always doing, preferring rather to do too much, which he sometimes did, than to do too little. Besides, his work was of a kind that almost any one single department of it was enough to give full occupation to the powers of an ordinary man;

yet he so attended to each, that none was neglected, and in all he attained to influence and distinction. For this he was singularly favoured in many ways, but in this one particularly and to a marvellous degree—that he could pass without distraction, and as if refreshed by the bare fact of transition, from one fatiguing employment to another, through a long day and a long succession of days, manifesting the same aptitude for each, and preserving the same cheerfulness through the whole. An aged minister, the Rev. W. Shuttleworth, thus writes of him: "I was his neighbour once, for some years; and I well remember that I had often the impression that I had never known a gentleman who seemed more providentially placed to be a blessing to a neighbourhood, as a citizen and a Christian; and he felt and acted as both. His country and the church were constantly upon his heart, and shared no little in his active effort and life. He was everywhere, and in everything that was praiseworthy, and calculated to benefit man and to glorify God. He was a patriot, a philanthropist, a Christian. This activity often excited my astonishment, considering his multifarious personal avocations connected with the manufactory and his large private business. I never knew an individual more industrious, both early and late. It was wonderful. And then applications to him for advice, &c., in personal and family matters, arrangement of plans and adjustment of difficulties, throughout the entire neighbourhood, were almost endless. Mr. John was the man of the people in cases and changes of all kinds. I can recollect times, not a few, when I have had to wait hours for such kinds of application before I could prefer my suit, or confer on my business. And then, withal, as soon as he passed his office door and entered his house, his mind was as free as if nothing was upon it but the occurrence then and there transpiring. He was instantly your friend, and business appeals, directions, and other concernments, were all gone. I once spoke to Mrs. Ridgway of his freedom from business cares and of his cheerfulness, when waiting his arrival home. She remarked, we should find him cheerful when he came, though she knew he was greatly occupied, and had been from an early hour in the morning. She said she had never seen him otherwise at any time. He had always a smile for home, and seemed there, whatever his previous anxieties, cheerful and happy."

No one works so well as he who loves his work, and he who loves his work is mostly rewarded by it. The demand of the great Roman, " *Quis enim virtutem amplectitur ipsam, præmia si tollas?*"—

"take away the rewards of virtue, and who would then embrace it?" is sufficiently met by the common adage that "virtue is its own reward." What is true of virtue is equally true of work, when the work is worthy, and the love for it sincere; for in fact work and virtue are in this case very much the same thing. Yet since there are other rewards to be had besides this essential one, who has so just a right to them as he that does the most, or works the best? It is he, be assured, who for the most part gets them; for there is a secret law controlling all other laws; a fixed operation of Divine Providence shaping and directing all other operations, which steadily tends to this result. And yet there are notable exceptions to the contrary, though fewer it may be than men's mistaken estimate of themselves would be willing to allow. These are found chiefly in the bestowment of civil honours, and such rewards as come in acknowledgment of services rendered to the public. Rewards of this kind are commonly in the hands of men who have the power to serve themselves and their friends, and who, if without any strong disposition to do this, have yet a party to please, or a predilection to gratify. If the state bestows them, the state thinks first of those who are most pledged to its support.

Opposition to any of its great institutions is a reason for neglect, for restricted right and civil disadvantage even, whatever the personal merit may be. Hence dissent from the Established Church (though one should think that faith and worship, having relation to things divine, should be as free as possible from secular legislation), is marked by peculiar discouragement. Time was when it knew little else than suffering, and when it suffered many things. In days yet more favourable it had much more of penalty than of privilege; while even now every concession that is won for it is won by oft-repeated and most resolute struggle. Still a far more equitable spirit is abroad, and a far more equitable spirit sits and rules in high places than formerly. A difference of faith is not now ostensibly the ground of partiality in legislative enactment, or social standing; and though the principle of a perfect equality, as between the churchman and the dissenter, still wants something to a complete and final recognition, and must want this so long as the state unites to itself, for peculiar distinction and privilege, one of the several sections of the Church of Christ in this land; yet many a wall of separation between the two has been thrown down, many a restrictive landmark has been swept away, and, if not always in practice, yet mostly in theory, the offices and honours open to one are accessible to the other.

Mr. Ridgway was a conscientious Dissenter in religion, as he was an enlightened Reformer in politics. Many must have been his temptations to forsake his early religious associations, had his dissent been less a matter of principle. Much sooner it may be, but for this, would his public character and services have received some honourable acknowledgment from those who were able to give it than they did, while the acknowledgment itself would probably have been more ample and gratifying than it was. Gratifying, indeed, we must still think it, especially as given to one whose political and religious sentiments were so decided and outspoken; as given also unsolicited, and in sheer recognition of claims which even prejudice and partizanship were constrained to speak of as very much more than ordinary. Among other distinctions conferred upon him, the value of which was increased by the circumstances attending them, was that of being made magistrate of the borough in which he resided, magistrate of the county of Stafford, and deputy lieutenant of the same. How much these honours were the reward of conspicuous merit, and bestowed for its sake, may be judged of by one of several similar communications. It is as follows:—

"Teddesby, Nov. 13th, 1853.

"My dear Sir,—I have thought, ever since I was Lord Lieutenant, of proposing to you to allow me to put you in the Commission of the Peace for this county. I am now pressed to make some additional appointments for Hanley and Shelton, and I take the liberty of asking whether, if you are appointed, you would qualify to act in these Townships. Your personal character, and your position in the Pottery District, leave no doubt in my mind that your appointment as a magistrate would be generally approved of. I must add that, from a very long standing friendship with you, it would be particularly agreeable to me to do any act that would be agreeable to yourself.

"I remain,
"My dear Sir,
"Yours faithfully,
"Hatherton.

"J. Ridgway, Esq.

"P.S.—My own opinion has long been that the peace and security of society in your district would be much promoted by its receiving municipal organization."

Accordingly, a charter of incorporation was obtained, under the leadership of Mr. Ridgway, and he himself, by common preference, became the first Mayor.

These honours were not accepted as rewards for the past, but as enlistments for the future—not as decorations to be worn in token of service already performed, but as opportunities furnished, and pledges taken for other service yet to be rendered. Into every additional appointment he carried a new sense of responsibility, and delighted in it chiefly as a fresh channel into which his inexhaustible activity could be usefully turned.

One distinction, which was purely honorary, involving neither office nor duty of any kind, save as everything does which adds to our reputation or influence, he is said to have declined. "He is said:" I put it thus, not from any doubt of the circumstance, but from the absence of documentary evidence. "On two separate occasions," says his nephew, who lived with him as a son, "the honour of knighthood was offered him by influential parties, in some way connected with the government, who had good reason for knowing that the title would be conferred." This testimony has other authentication quite as reliable. Indeed the offer is now one of the traditions of the Pottery towns. For many years it has been accepted without question, and occasionally, when popular feeling has boiled over, under some political or other excitement, the title itself has been given him to spice a jest, or point a sarcasm. Why then did he not accept it? "I once ventured to ask him," writes the Rev. C. D. Ward, "and he gave this reply:—'It would have placed another step between me and my Christian friends, and made me, in their view, less approachable. There is social distance enough already, and too much; and I could accept no honour that would sever me from my brethren in Christ.'" This could hardly have been the only reason; the less so as the consequence hinted at was by no means a necessary consequence; and still further, as Mr. Ridgway was certainly not more insensible to honour than the generality of his class. It may be—this indeed has been asserted—that he esteemed the proffered distinction too lightly to make it an object of desire.

In the absence of all other honour Mr. Ridgway had honour enough in his work; if not, he was undeserving of all honour whatever. "An energetic nature," says Goethe, "feels itself brought into the world for its own development, and not for the approbation of the public." Such a nature, pervaded and controlled by the spirit of a true benevolence, stops not even here, but regards this very development as the means to something further;

the well-being of others. While again, a nature thus endowed, but in addition, renewed by the grace of the Gospel, mounts still higher, and carries every inferior motive into that highest of all motives—a supreme desire to do the will of God. What to such a nature is the mere "approbation of the public," considered as an end of action? And what are the distinctions which society, or even sovereignty can confer, considered as a recompence for it? Trifling indeed, as compared with the rewards which spring from the work itself—from the cause of philanthropy, or from the service of God. What greater honour can a man wish for than simply to be employed in either of these? What higher distinction can he have than to take a lead in each, and especially with so much influence as to draw multitudes after him in the same course? What richer reward can he covet than to know, that in neither has he laboured in vain, but rather with much success? All this Mr. Ridgway had; and if he desired more, he had, consciously or unconsciously, as much as a reasonable ambition could crave, not only in the honours professedly bestowed in acknowledgment of his public services by those who had such honours to give, but in the generous esteem of a large constituency of admiring friends and fellow labourers; in the testimony so demonstratively borne to his merits by the district in which he lived on his retirement from business; in the surprise and almost consternation of grief, which smote the Pottery towns on the announcement of his sudden death; in the tribute then spontaneously paid to his worth by those who had held a different creed from himself, whether in politics or religion; in the sorrow that sat on such a vast assemblage of countenances on the day of his burial, and which accompanied him, or all which death had had any power over, in such mournful but imposing procession to the grave. What beyond this is possible, he doubtless now enjoys in that more perfect state, where even a cup of cold water given here, if rightly given, meets with a due reward.

CHAPTER VIII.

The Faith kept, the Course finished.

CHAPTER VIII.

THE FAITH KEPT, THE COURSE FINISHED.

Mr. Ridgway might have sat for the charming portrait of "A Green Old Age," so exquisitely drawn by Mr. Binney, in his justly popular work, "Is it possible to make the best of both Worlds?" He might indeed have sat for the whole chapter, suggesting most of "the constituent elements of a satisfactory and beautiful form of life in the present world," which enter into its theory. In him the theory was realized with a most exemplary completeness, making the reality "a refreshing and a beautiful sight." There were health, cheerfulness, competence, reputation, some considerable culture of the intellect and the affections—all ripened and mellowed in a green old age.

"It is delightful," says Mr. Binney, in his portraiture of this last constituent element, "to see a man who, having passed the previous stage of life with credit and honour, approaches the last, and goes through it with contentment and cheerfulness. Look at him. There's a good deal of many of his wonted attributes about him yet; force in his intellect, freshness in his feelings, light in his eye, and vigour in his limbs! He reviews the past without pain and without complaint. He is not querulous, selfish, misanthropic. He does not confound and frighten the young by constantly telling them of "the howling wilderness" into which they have been born, and of the wretched thing they will find life to be. He has not found it anything of the sort. The world has proved to him a very pleasant place, and life an interesting though eventful journey. Life did not turn out, perhaps, just what he fancied and dreamt about as a boy, or even as a man; it became a rougher, but withal a better and nobler thing. He does not therefore attempt to touch too rudely the dreams of the young enthusiasts about him. He listens to them with interest and pleasure;—sometimes with a significant but loving silence, sometimes answering and encouraging with genial sympathy. He does not destroy their hopes and anticipations, for while he feels that they will be probably fulfilled in a way somewhat different from what is projected, he feels also that they may *be* fulfilled, and that life may become to his successors what it has been to him. His hoary head is a crown of glory; his name fragrant as incense. He stands the centre of a large and widening circle of descendants:—children and children's children gather about him."*

This last feature in the picture, drawn out by the author into some detail, and made very striking in its familiar beauty, was wanting in our otherwise closely resembling reality. Mr. Ridgway was not the centre of a large and widening circle of descendants. If "children's children are," as Solomon says they are, "the crown of old men," then that was a crown which was never platted or gemmed for him. He had never the privilege of gathering about him a group of bright merry little creatures, and of realizing the charming fancy of Mr. Binney, by saying with exultant joy—"There's a fine fellow! that's my son's boy! and see here, this is my daughter's little girl! Bless the dears! I am quite proud of them." He had not the pleasure preliminary to this, of seeing his hearth crowded with children of his own, and of living over again in their tender innocence and sportive merriment the days of his own childhood, or of looking forward, in the pro-

* *"Is it possible to make the best of both Worlds?"*—Pp. 38, 39.

mise of their unfolding loveliness, and growing intelligence and virtue, to a yet greater joy in the future than had been his joy in the past. He had not even one such, whom, receiving as "an heritage from the Lord," he could religiously train for Him, and so, in due time, find his own life doubled in the maturing life of his child. Still his hearth was not lonely, for other children were there, scattering sunshine around them, and filling the domestic atmosphere with the music of their mirth; children, whom an early orphanage had cast wholly on his care, and whom the memory of a sister, now lost but ever beloved, had made it a solemn pleasure to watch over and to nurture. Nor indeed in their absence would his home have been solitary, but still the sanctuary of sweet and tender charities, and therefore of sweet and tender joys; for *she* was there whose presence could ever make it so. We have seen how he loved her; at least, we have seen how much he must have loved her. The proof abounds in the diary from which, in a previous chapter, some extracts have been taken; but abounds much more, and much more strikingly, than in these extracts it appears. "My Sophia" is met with continually, on almost every page of the hundreds of pages he wrote; certainly in every day's record, as if it were a pleasure merely to write her name. She is never forgotten in his Sabbath meditations, and is never absent from his morning and evening prayer. The thought of her is present unceasingly, in travel or at rest, mingling with other thoughts where it does not stand alone; now operating through fear for her safety, yet fear passing immediately into confidence of God's loving protection; again taking the form of devout solicitude for her spiritual well-being, especially as the season for social or public worship comes round; always revealing itself in a feeling of exile and loneliness, combined at the same time with eager and yearning anticipations of an early and happy reunion.

The love thus evinced was no transient love, or occasional; was not dependent for any actual strength of it on the exceptional circumstance of a long and distant absence from home, though to this circumstance, doubtless, we owe the frequent and permanent record of it. The record itself is but as a single expression of a life-long experience, but as a momentary glimpse of that which continues onward the same to the end. This love, returned by her who was the object of it as freely as it was given, made home anything but solitary. Habitual cheerfulness reigned there, and if sorrow entered, it was so exclusively for others that it only enhanced their own proper joy. Each living for

T

the other, and both living to God, their domestic life was equally beautiful and blessed. Beautiful it was in its elegant retirement and uniform tranquillity, as never failing in those delicate attentions and graceful courtesies, which are apt to evaporate in the familiarity which the cynical proverb says breeds contempt; but which, as marking each day's intercourse, are ever the sure proof that mutual love is grounded in mutual esteem. There was almost, indeed, a formality and studied courtliness in their behaviour to each other. Blessed it was by that which rendered it beautiful; and still more, because their mutual love was exalted into something of a religious principle, and sanctified by the love of Christ. Thus it continued for many years, more than are usually vouchsafed to mortals, and with fewer of those "days of darkness," which come in upon the summer life of every household; flowing gently on in its own sweet and self-sufficing privacy, "like"—to adapt Coleridge's beautiful image — "a hidden brook, that in the leafy month of June, singeth a quiet tune."

But it could not be thus always: nor would faith have it so. At best the season of sorrow is only postponed, as winter is sometimes late in coming; but the law which appoints it cannot in any case be broken, or in any lose its effect.

Providence may grant a respite from one or more of its own trying ordinances, but it never allows a complete exemption. Singular in its mercy is that appointment of Heaven, by which a man is privileged to live joyfully with the wife of his youth until the shadows of threescore years and ten begin to gather about him; but the mercy surely ceases, or rather veils itself in that which it is not so easy to recognise as mercy: the inevitable decree which cuts asunder all earthly ties comes forth at last, leaving him, it may be, not only bereaved, but quite alone. Thus was it with him whose course we have now followed to this prescribed boundary of human existence, and thus was it at the time when this boundary was all but in sight. With what effect the stroke lighted few were permitted to know, as few had known how much love there was to wound, and how much happiness to wither. He did not obtrude his sorrow, as before he had not paraded his joy. The "brook" was "hidden," I have said, and its sweet murmur had been but little heard at a distance. The "garden" was "enclosed," to use Solomon's figure, and, when the blight passed over it, hardly anyone could tell how much beauty had been scattered or fragrance wasted. The less so as Mr. Ridgway sought immediate relief to his pain in labours which called off his thoughts from himself to others, as also in the society of Christian friends, whose private fellowship he courted now more than previously, as if to fill up the space on his hearth made vacant and desolate by his loss. Moreover, faith came quickly with its ministries of heavenly consolation, especially with its reconciling assurance that the dispensation was the Lord's, and as such must be both wise and good; while hope, looking with strong vision through the clear light of a divine revelation into a future unspeakably more glorious than the present, found solace, and even more than solace, in the anticipation of that final "gathering together unto Him," which is to crown and perpetuate in a now unknown blessedness the earthly endearments of those who in this world have "dwelt together according to knowledge, as being heirs together of the grace of life."

The following brief replies to two or three of the many letters of respectful sympathy written to him in his bereavement, by ministers of various churches and friends of different classes, from Members of Parliament downward, reveal something of his state of mind—his affliction, his submission, his consolation — at this season of trial. The first two are addressed to the Rev. W. Mills, who had himself just passed through a similar probation of suffering; the other to the

Rev. P. J. Wright, both ministers with whom he was on terms of friendly intercourse.

"Cauldon Place, Dec. 5, 1854.

"MY DEAR SIR,—Your letter of sympathy has been like healing balm, and as the refreshing rain. Your example has so fully prepared my way for Christian resignation, that I have only had to remember to follow it. And now your exhortation encourages me to receive this dispensation as at the hand of God, and to adore that hand, though it has smitten me. I do trust in Him, for He is worthy. He is my refuge, for He is faithful; and He shall have my heart and life, that living or dying I may be His. My dear wife has passed many years of bodily suffering: nor have I been without my share of suffering on her account, and, indeed, on my own, lest my case should be peculiar, and so be misinterpreted by me. But hers was the lot, and mine also, to endure with patience the trials appointed, and to leave the rest with God. Amidst all she loved religion, and the people of God, and knew the grace of God in Christ. Her mind sank much under this affliction, particularly since the attack of paralysis; but she bore the chastening with meekness, and breathed her last in peace. On Friday we shall inter her remains at Bethesda. May I trouble you to conduct such a service as was observed at your dear wife's interment?

"I remain, my dear sir,
"Faithfully yours,
"Jno. Ridgway."

"Cauldon Place, Dec. 13, 1854.

"My dear Sir,—On looking over many consolatory notes, I find yours of the 5th inst., and thank you for it. That was a day most eventful to me, since I then sustained a great loss, though my departed wife realized a greater gain. Most submissively do I bow to the dispensation, praying that all its gracious ends may be answered, and God glorified in me and by me. I am so often looking for my poor wife, that at present I am restless and confused. It will take some time before things past are forgotten, and the mind is reconciled to the change which has taken place. In the meantime, I am casting my care on Him who careth for me, and who I know will sustain me.

"Affectionately yours,
"Jno. Ridgway."

"Cauldon Place, Dec. 14, 1854.

"My dear Friend,—I thank you for your friendly and welcome letter, than which nothing could be more seasonable. I have indeed sustained a great loss, and I do and shall feel it for life. But though I mourn, I submit, and meekly say, "Father, thy will be done." I have to be thankful for many years' joys—that the cord has been quietly but perceptibly loosing—that I have been able to administer much consolation, and that my beloved wife has quietly slept in Jesus. I cannot wish her return to the land of mortality. I am journeying to meet her in a better land, where there is neither sickness nor death. Thank God for His promises and His Son, for His Spirit and His grace, for the joys of religion here, and the glories of eternal life hereafter. And I trust that you and I, and our tribes, will be found amongst the glorious multitude before the throne. My best regards to your wife, family, and friends.

And am, dear sir,
"Faithfully yours,
"Jno. Ridgway."

In one of the preceding letters Mr. Ridgway speaks of suffering on his own account, as well as on account of his wife; but this suffering must have been chiefly of that general kind which implies no particular disease, which grows out of sympathy with another who suffers directly and specifically, and increases as the affliction is prolonged by the strain and tension which love in self-forgetfulness willingly undergoes in the sufferer's behalf. Of real bodily affliction—the affliction which racks with pain or consumes by slow degrees till life has all but ebbed away, laying aside from daily occupations and confining to home in utter helplessness—he had known but little; or if a little—for who indeed can hope or even rationally desire to be wholly exempt?—yet assuredly less than falls to the lot of most. As little had he known of that continuing sickliness and feebleness which to some make life, even though long, a long disease; and which, though it does not prevent the doing of much work and the achievement of noble designs, because the will is strong and the innate force of the mind great enough to triumph over the incapacity of the body, imparting to it something of its own secret strength, yet renders the achievement a labour and a task, rewarded, it may be, by the solemn pleasure springing from a consciousness of duty, but seldom relieved and brightened by that exhilarating glow of animal spirit—that warm flush of bounding joy suffusing the whole man,—which makes it a privilege to live. Even age found him almost without its customary infirmities; there was not much more than the slightest perceptible shadow of these upon him, while in spirit he was nearly as buoyant as in youth. The great Latin poet, in lines much admired by Dr. Johnson, says:—

> "Optima quæque dies miseris mortalibus ævi
> Prima fugit: subeunt morbi, tristisque senectus:
> Et labor, et duræ rapit inclementia mortis."*

Thus rendered by Dryden:—

> "In youth alone, unhappy mortals live;
> But, ah! the mighty bliss is fugitive:
> Discolour'd sickness, anxious labour, come,
> And age, and death's inexorable doom."

Melancholy is this picture of human life, which thus places happiness in the early part of it only, describing it as a succession of experiences in which the best come first, but speedily vanish, and are afterwards followed by disease, toil, sorrowful old age, and unwelcome death. This picture surely belongs to the meridian of heathenism only, or but slightly to that of Christianity. In so far as it *does* belong to this latter,—as in some of its features it does and must, since these are characteristically human,—it applies to the subject of our memoir with a considerable modification of the common experience. To him the best part of life was not the beginning, nor the middle; not religiously, not intellectually, nor, save in

* Virgil's Georgics, III. 66.

some abridgment of former activity and capability of endurance, even bodily. Old age to him was not sad, much less morose; it was not a sorrowful winter, but a bright, rich, mellow autumn, and an autumn, too, into which summer had been far prolonged. He was one of the very few to whom youth seems given as a perpetual dowry, with at the same time the power to live in every consecutive period, and to gather the wisdom peculiar to each. He appears to have been conscious of something of this kind himself, at least of a perennial freshness which withstood in a singular degree the ordinary encroachments of time, for, when he was seventy-three years of age, being spoken of in a meeting for religious business as " our *venerable* friend, Mr. Ridgway," he was eager to decline the intended compliment, saying in reply, that " that was a thing he had yet to hope for."

A year or two after the death of his wife, however, an infirmity producing temporary lameness came upon him; nor lameness only, which, as interrupting his labours, was severe enough, but at times also most acute suffering. His previous experience having in so small a degree prepared him for this, he felt it, as almost any one unaccustomed to affliction would, to be a very painful trial. Besides, in the confinement to which it doomed him, it reopened the wound which his late domestic loss had occasioned, and by throwing him upon others, whether strangers or kindred, for those manifold attentions which the sympathetic love of *one* would have made healing in their very tenderness, it gave him a more exquisite sense of the bereavement he had suffered. The thought of this bereavement made a protracted illness a distressing anticipation. It cast a gloom upon the future which sometimes made the present gloomy, particularly at those times when faith for a moment was foiled in the conflict with sense, and the flow of religious consolation was restrained by the acuteness of bodily anguish, just as the inflowing tide is held in check by the violence of an opposing wind. The prospect of suffering is dreary enough in itself, but the prospect of *loneliness* in suffering—of no fellowship of domestic sympathy and no succours of a watchful and gently ministering love—especially with recollections of such a fellowship once happily enjoyed, and now vivified to a feeling of irreparable loss, together with the consciousness of age which a younger experience, however willing to humour or console, might not be able to understand, and the further consciousness of dependence for the ordinary alleviations of sickness, if not absolutely on strangers, yet for the most part on servants—this surely is dreariness made still more drear. But apart from this, as it would have been to Mr. Ridgway an affliction of some severity to be simply arrested in his unceasing and multiplied labours, so it was an element of peculiar aggravation to the affliction he positively endured, that it consigned him to silence, and compelled him literally to do nothing.

The affliction, however, though painful, was profitable, and felt to be so. It proved to be one of those merciful, though *naturally* unwelcome, ordeals through which the great Purifier sometimes conducts His people, and during which, as indeed it is for this purpose the operation itself takes place,—

> " The dross is purged
> Away, below ; and in the liquid metal,
> Perfect and pure through suffering, the Finer,
> Looking therein, sees his own image clear
> Reflected : and the holy workmanship
> Of every feature, by his art divine,
> He fixes there, never to be effaced."*

This result was manifest during the continuance of the affliction, and still more afterwards. The strong man was bowed down. The will, ordinarily so self-asserting and resolute, was subdued to such a gentle and easy pliancy, that his "soul was even as a weaned child." Tears were often the proof of his tenderness, showing how

* Aird.

deeply the fountains of his nature were broken up. These were tears sometimes of sorrow, more frequently of thankfulness, and yet, perhaps, still oftener of that mingled experience in which several emotions unite, as past, present, and future come into view. The Word of God, ever, as we have seen, "the man of his counsel," had almost a new tongue, certainly a new sweetness to him. Nothing was more welcome to him, nothing so welcome, as religious conversation and prayer. During these exercises I have seen him moved to deep excitement, the strong currents of feeling as they coursed along shaking visibly his whole frame. And this gracious state remained. The fruit was seen afterwards, and ever afterwards, ripening and mellowing continually, until the whole was ready for the gathering. In reply to a communication from the Rev. P. J. Wright, after his return home from Cheltenham, whither a search for health had taken him, he writes:—" I thank you most unaffectedly for all your kind expressions of Christian sympathy and goodwill, because I know them to be as genuine as they are acceptable. And now, allow me to say, I returned home on Saturday last, just as a schoolboy would return home at the holidays; and indeed, my dear friend, I have been at school, and, though a suffering, be assured it has been a salutary one;

so that I bless God for it, and pray that the discipline may be sanctified in my greater conformity to His will. My health is very much better, and my poor limb nearly healed, although weak and requiring careful attention. This, with the help of God, I shall give, and so relax my concerns as to keep within compass; making shorter days, longer nights; less for the world, and more for the church and for heaven. I am sure you will agree with me that this will do." . . . . .

"A long letter for an invalid," as he himself calls it, concludes with this brief etching of present experience: "But I must say, I had a delightful Sunday at Bethesda, under the Word, and with God's people. The ordinance of the Lord's Supper was to me the very Gate of Heaven."

"Less for the world, and more for the church and for heaven,"—this was henceforth to be the maxim of his life. But little time remained for its observance. In four short years the heaven for which he had determined thus to live was to be gained. A longer period of preparation might have been expected; a longer period was by himself anticipated. But the promise of to-day, or what is taken for promise, is seldom realized by the event of to-morrow. To-morrow, indeed, is wholly shut out from our view, and can be seen by no eye but His to whom the present and the future are as one. "God is greater than man: Why dost thou strive against Him? For He giveth not account of any of His matters." What is written in the book of His providence cannot be read until, by the hand of time, the page is turned towards us. The maxim, however, was not only kept in mind, but was almost as much observed as though Mr. Ridgway had himself been permitted to turn the page, and to read, in its appointed place, the secret entry, "This year thou shalt die." It is thus in truth God often prepares His servants, by a leading of which at the time they are unconscious, for some important event which lies immediately, though unseen, before them; especially for that one event which, while the most solemn of all, is also the last of all. They go towards it as if by a steady direction of purpose; or rather are drawn towards it as though by some mysterious attraction, half felt but not understood, arising from its close and continually increasing proximity.

The first part of the maxim—"less for the world"—was acted upon at once and decisively, by a purpose to retire from business. The step when taken was one of public interest. Such a man, and such a manufacturer, could not be allowed to relinquish the position he had occupied for so many years, even in connexion with the trade of the district, without some proof of the esteem in which he was held by the town in general, and some further proof of the esteem of his own workpeople. We have seen how in both cases this esteem was testified; though we have not seen, and may not see, how much genuine goodwill the testimony embodied and represented. But, however interesting to the public, the step was one, we must think, of much greater interest to Mr. Ridgway himself. Perhaps it was the realization of hopes which had been entertained from the beginning of his commercial life, but which, sharing the ordinary fortunes of human hopes, had alternately risen and fallen, just as prosperities or reverses had come to cheer or check them. The goal is undoubtedly one to be desired, provided it be made a new starting-point to something further and higher. Most business men probably have it in view, though few gain it, or even expect to gain it; while of those who succeed, a very small number really enjoy what it is supposed to give. The object is not unlawful, nor unworthy to be aimed at. That need not be a man's "treasure," of which nevertheless he has been permitted to lay up some considerable amount in the present life. He may, notwithstanding its daily accumulations, have esteemed other things, and especially the "one thing," unspeakably more highly than this earthly good, and have employed it, with a liberality proportioned to its increase, in their pursuit and service. Besides, repose comes naturally after toil, and may surely be prolonged when no further need of toil exists. Retirement on a competency which exempts from labour, at least from the fear of want, is the fitting reward of a long career of honourable industry. We like to watch the evening close in thus peacefully upon him whose day has been vexed by cloud and tempest, or whose unresting activity has found for each succeeding hour employment that has taxed his powers to the full. It is pleasant to see age retiring from the competitions and fatigues of business, and going quietly down into the valley, flooded with the rich light of the descending sun, to enjoy in well-earned leisure and placid contentment the fruit of the vineyard which its own hands have planted.

And yet, if enjoyment alone be the object, it is rarely found, or soon exhausted. The first few draughts may be agreeable, but a continuance of the same thing weakens the relish, and in the end becomes distasteful. It is within the observation of everyone, that individuals having made a fortune out of trade, and choosing for the rest of their lives to enjoy what they have made, soon grow tired and sick at heart with their new position, relieving its tedium often by excitement and change, which prove as dangerous to their future interests, as they are ruinous to their present. Cicero says, *Si vero habet aliquod tanquam pabulum studii atque doctrinæ, nihil est otiosa senectute jucundius :** that is, nothing is more pleasant than a leisurely old age, providing there is pabulum—food for the employment and gratification of the intellect. But, unhappily, to most merchants and manufacturers who have succeeded in amassing wealth sufficient to give them ease in their declining years, this condition is wanting. The intellectual pabulum is not there; or if it is, the intellectual appetite is not. They have been accustomed for the most part to other diet, and cannot readily so far change their habit as to find enjoyment in this. Besides, enjoyment itself is no great or worthy object for which to live. It is to be had as a result, not sought for as an end. There is nothing noble in the search, because there is something selfish; nor any certainty even that the search will lead to what is desired. The certainty rather is that in most cases it will not; for pleasure, like the horizon, recedes from him who pursues it, and, like the *ignis fatuus*, tempts to danger where the pursuit is thoughtless and eager. Enjoyment comes from the right direction and

* "De Senectute," c. 14.

exercise of man's faculties, and the highest enjoyment from that which is highest in these. There must be work, or there cannot be any enjoyment at all, save as this results from a momentary intoxication of the senses; and the work must be noble—a resolute performance of well-understood duty, in which the happiness of others is concerned as well as our own—or the enjoyment can never rise to a true blessedness. Hence retirement from business must be simply a change of occupation, a higher kind of activity taking the place of that which is lower; otherwise leisure becomes idleness, and leisure combined with luxury leads to corruption. "A useless life," it has been beautifully said, " is a premature death."*
The man degenerates, virtually decays, and dies *as* man, who has no object to live for that carries him out of himself. His very blessings turn to curses, as if in revenge for their non-improvement. The wealth, previously accumulated by hard labour, fails to be a joy to him; or, what is still worse, becomes his only joy. His riches corrupt, and his garments are moth-eaten. His gold and silver canker, and in the end the rust thereof is a witness against him, and eats his flesh as it were fire.

The true corollary therefore of the maxim, " less

* Ein unnütz Leben ist ein früher Tod.—Goethe. "Iphigenia auf Tauris."

for the world," is, "more for the church and for heaven." The two parts make up one complete rule of conduct, which in declining years it is beautiful to see observed. There is not only fitness and propriety in the rule, but the exemplification of it in actual life gives us one of the noblest sights which earth has to present. If it is pleasant to follow age into private, and to observe it, after years of incessant toil in worldly business, in dignified possession of ease and quiet, it is more than pleasant, it is a positive delight, because a reverend and beautiful thing, to see it, with powers hardly impaired by time, with wisdom ripened by experience, and gains on which no rust of wrong has been able to gather, consecrated wholly to the service of Christ and His church, withholding no talent that can be used, and finding in spiritual things the complete employment of energies that have hitherto been given to things temporal: and then to see the effect of all this in the softening to a purely Christian mould of those harsher features which the strifes of commercial business are apt to develope or exaggerate, in the subjugation of the will and temper to a childlike teachableness and simplicity, in the mellowing and perfecting of the whole character, giving it the richness and glory as of some spiritual autumn; and thus, by this growing separation from the world, and deepening communion with God, realizing in the end what was so finely said of one of our great English confessors,* that while on earth he lived so near to heaven, that when he died he had not far to go.

But a short time, comparatively, was permitted to Mr. Ridgway to observe this second part of his maxim. He did less for the church and for heaven than he had intended; less than he had formally set himself to do. To his own eye his life lengthened out into the perspective of several years to come. Nevertheless, he did not postpone, but commenced his additional work at once. The dark valley was nearer than he thought. Its solemn shadows were lengthening towards him, because his sun was going rapidly down. And though he saw the sun rather than the shadows, yet he lived as though he equally beheld them both. The hand of God was secretly leading him away from the world, and he followed its leading, as though sensible of its pressure. The relief obtained from secular business was given to strictly religious duties, or to duties into which the spirit of religion was more persistently carried. The effect of this was soon apparent to others, as indeed it was soon felt by himself. Invisible things became more consciously real, and eternal

* Ridley.

things more consciously near. A peculiar softness took possession of him which made him singularly quick and sensitive to their influence, so that he seemed to apprehend them as by a new sense of their importance and power. This softness extended to his intercourse with friends and opponents, manifesting itself in a conciliatory gentleness of disposition and manner, which, in former times, was sometimes wanting, and over the want of which he had often mourned. It also affected, by rendering more susceptible, his naturally and now habitually generous affections and sympathies, giving to his charities a wider channel and a deeper current. It operated to a still higher result, by purifying to a holier sensibility and stimulating to a livelier zeal that compassion for sinners, and desire for their spiritual well-being, which is never absent from a soul truly converted to God. This compassion appeared in many ways, and in every relation in which he stood to the church and the world. It made him, as a magistrate, what a magistrate is ordained to be, the minister of God for good; especially in this sense, that, desiring rather to prevent than to punish, he strove to stem the torrent of corruption by drying up its springs; to arrest the progress of crime and social wretchedness, by diminishing the means to their promotion and increase; and thus to prepare the way, in the removal of obstructions which most impede its course, for the freer access of the Gospel to those who from the depth of their degradation stand in the greatest need of it. It led him, as an ordinary Christian labourer, to pursue this work still further; not only in the use of means that had become habitual, but in the choice of others that were special; as, for instance, by sometimes seeking an interview with the wrongdoer, even when the wrongdoing had exposed him to legal penalties, by addressing words of admonition and counsel to the idle and depraved—to most of whom he was well known—as he passed on the Sabbath to and from the house of God, or by delivering to them religious tracts, of which he not unfrequently provided himself with a store, in the hope that, although scattered by the wayside, the seed would in some instances fall into good ground.

Intensely anxious was he for the prosperity of the church to which he belonged. This object, always dear to him, was now dearer than ever. The prosperity wished for was numerical increase by means of conversion. To him no other prosperity was sufficiently real and demonstrative, while yet other prosperity was valued both as the means to this, and as precious on its own account. He craved for visible results. His desire for these

grew almost to a passion. It was not enough that
means were used; these must have some calculable
success. It was well to vindicate the truth against
cavil; it was better to smite the conscience with
conviction. It was allowable to exhibit the Gospel in clear and masterly exposition; but the end
was missed, or only partially gained, where it did
not prove the power of God unto salvation. It
was a small thing so to preach the Word that
men must praise the talent displayed; it was a
great thing, and the only thing really wanted, so
to preach it that they must receive the message
delivered. What availed it to have expressions of
admiration from those who heard? But it availed
much—more than could be told—to have from the
broken and burdened heart the cry, "Sirs, what
must I do to be saved?" This feeling was towards
the last encouraged, if such a thing can be,
almost to excess. Though it never seduced him
into the error of those who find a ready explanation of the want of numerical increase in some
palpable defect in him who preaches the Gospel;
though it never carried him to the length of
depreciating any one of the several kinds of
ministry by which the common cause is served
(he knew the importance of that Divine ordination which secures to the Church a "diversity of
gifts" too well for that), yet it led him ultimately

perhaps to a too exclusive preference for that preaching which is most highly stimulating to the feelings; or if not (for it must be allowed that the preaching which does not reach the feelings, is like unskilful gunnery, that misses the object by shortness of range or indirectness of aim), it yet fostered a too craving desire for the employment of agencies and means additional to the ordinary ones, and which, because extraordinary and exceptional, should be reserved for occasions of extraordinary and exceptional necessity.

But in the zeal which longs for the salvation of sinners, a much graver error than this, if error it be thought, may well be pardoned. It is not excess of feeling, or even misdirection of effort resulting therefrom, that the Church has generally to mourn over: it is instead of this the lukewarmness that scarcely feels at all, and the indifference that deems every effort a burden. Only therefore let the zeal be genuine, and there is hardly any extent or any expression of it that will not rather be a good than an evil. Wildfire, it is sometimes said, is better than no fire at all; but fire kindled from the altar has little tendency to grow wild, and only does so when fed by unholy hands. Genuine zeal has in its very nature it own safeguard and commendation: always pursuing ends most worthy, it is sure, as a rule, to select methods most rightful and true. That such was Mr. Ridgway's zeal is evidenced by his whole life, as also by some of the last words he ever wrote. In a letter addressed to the Rev. Dr. Cooke, the day before his death, he says, "I have written to the Annual Committee about simultaneous prayer meetings, to be held in the first week in January, and I hope they may be made Connexional. We have a special meeting of our Society at Bethesda, on Monday evening, for free conversation, exhortation, and prayer. I hope the Master will be powerfully present with us. We want the Spirit poured out from on high, and some men of earnestness and zeal to carry out the purpose of His grace. We are too stiff and formal, and must get out of this unprofitable way; or, so far from extending, we shall narrow and decline. I say, may God have mercy upon us, and cause His face to shine upon us, and make His way known to us, and give us the desire of our hearts, even abundant prosperity."

It was one of the modes chosen for the profitable employment of his leisure, to visit a number of the societies of the Connexion in different parts of the kingdom, for the purpose of encouraging or stimulating to some needful work—to suggest new projects or help to further old ones, to assist by counsel at private gatherings, or by addresses and otherwise at public meetings. He had just finished a tour of this kind—the first formal one he had taken—intending, as he said, to "lay by for the winter," when the Master, whose "powerful presence" he was hoping for at a meeting "for free conversation and prayer" to be held in a few days, came in another sense than the one expected, yet came we may believe not unwelcomely, and suddenly but gently called him away from labour to rest. From labour: for the last day of his life was in this respect very much like other days, one of labour throughout. Nearly all kinds of labour were crowded into it; private and public, magisterial, philanthropic, and religious. And not until the day's work was done, and the night had fairly set in, did he cease to work. But then the cessation was final. The night knew no morrow, or the morrow came and John Ridgway "had another morn than ours."

His concluding work was to preside at a tea-meeting of the members of Bethesda Society. The occasion was congenial to his feelings, the object being to stimulate one another to increased activity in their Christian calling. Before me lies the order of business, prepared by himself, with his usual methodical precision, and bearing date the day of his decease. The topics of his own address also are given, and are good enough, as well as short enough, to be here transcribed. "If John Ridgway be chosen chairman, refer to his absence (Connexional tour), and the useful works going on. Then turn to home, and have a general talk of matters. Desire the friends to speak their views as to how the cause is getting on. Note specially brotherly love, Christian invitation, better visitation, more profitable prayer-meetings, better attention to the young, training them up for usefulness," &c. These and other topics were handled with more than his wonted animation and energy. A benignant cheerfulness lighted up his countenance, and a solemn earnestness pervaded his manner. The meeting took its tone from him, and this tone was sustained throughout. A deep spiritual joy seemed to have possession of all, so that all could sing at the close, he himself giving out the words, and singing more heartily than anyone else,

> "Together let us sweetly live,
> Together let us die;
> And each a starry crown receive,
> And reign above the sky."

A kindly "good night" separated him from friends whom he must never see again. With a buoyant step he returned home, his heart still vibrating with the pleasures of the evening. The threshold crossed, was crossed for the last time, but never before crossed with feelings harmonized to a deeper tranquillity than now. He sat down to rest, fatigued no doubt by the toils of the day, remarking to his attendant how greatly he had enjoyed the meeting. For a few seconds—they could hardly be minutes—she left him, to prepare his simple supper; and on her return was surprised to find him, as she thought, calmly asleep. Asleep he was, but the sleep was one from which the voice of the archangel and the trump of God alone was to wake him. The rest he had taken was rest for ever, the rest of the moment passing sweetly into the rest which remains for the people of God.

Very beautiful was this, notwithstanding its startling solemnity, because so complete a fulfilment of the Saviour's behest, "Occupy till I come." The pound was used to the last, and with so continuous an accumulation of interest, that we may well believe it had gained ten pounds. Fitting also was it as the termination of such a life as his; to which, from its previous laboriousness, any long period of inaction seemed as little to be desired for a close as, from its present solitariness, any long period of affliction. His removal was almost like a translation. He was not, for God took him. He did not see death, or he tasted it so little that the bitterness was but for a moment. There was hardly time for the dread messenger to present the cup, much less was there time consciously to drain it. The journey of life had brought him to the very brink of the river which separates the Wilderness from the Promised Land while yet he was capable of much further travel, and preparing for still additional achievements. He stood there without knowing it, and passed to the other side at once, not by wading the flood, but borne on angels' wings.

The day of interment was one not to be forgotten by those who witnessed the ceremony. The surprise, the consternation, the deep and painful sorrow produced by his sudden death in the immediate district, and in many other places to which his reputation had spread, particularly throughout the religious Denomination of which he had been so conspicuous a member, and which only increased during the several days succeeding up to that last one when the grave was to claim its kindred dust, found expression in a public demonstration which can only take place when the heart of a whole people is stirred with the sense of a common calamity and a common sympathy. The funeral was intended to be a private one, but the public grief demanded a public mourning. The corporation, magistrates, and town authorities generally, with various local associations and gentlemen of every shade of politics and every diversity of religious creed requested permission to testify their esteem of the departed, in being allowed to follow his remains to their final resting-place.

Mr. Ridgway died on the 3rd of December, 1860 : his interment took place seven days after. The morning was cold, damp, and gloomy, as if in sympathy with the occasion. A stranger on entering the town must have felt as though some great misfortune lay heavy upon it. Everything wore the appearance of sadness, and spoke the language of sorrow. The streets were silent, yet crowded. Business was generally suspended, as though the people had enough to do for one day at least to think of their recent loss. The manufactories were deserted. The shops were closed. The window-blinds were drawn in nearly every house. Even publicans and beersellers, who perhaps of all had least reason to put on any semblance of mourning for the deceased, seeing that when living he had shown himself but little friendly to their interests, were willing for a season to forego the profits of their trade, and, in appearance at least, to swell the tide of public grief. A more than Sabbath stillness, because a stillness without the Sabbath's cheerfulness, hung over the town, broken only, as also rendered more oppressive, by the measured chime of muffled bells, and by the sounding footsteps of numbers who were streaming from every direction towards the chapel in which the funeral service was to be conducted, or to some convenient point for observation in the road along which the funeral procession was to pass. These numbers swelled to thousands—to many thousands—massed together in vast assemblages of both sexes at those places in the route where the best view was thought to be had, and again stretching away in narrower lines for about the distance of a mile, forming one irregular but continuous avenue of human beings; all looking on in decorous silence, and not a few in tears that could not be restrained. Along this far-reaching vista moved slowly and solemnly on a multitudinous procession of kindred, neighbours, town officials, colleagues in public duty, members of local societies, ministers of different churches, friends Christian and political, with some formerly opponents, but now opponents no longer—all drawn together by the attraction of a common bereavement, and now united in the expression of a common admiration and regret.

Impressive beyond all description was the scene presented in the chapel—in "Bethesda"—the sanctuary so dear to him whose voice, now silent, but a few days before was heard in it mingling

with others in the high praises of God. Often
had his soul by devout participation in its services
been rapt to a very paradise of spiritual joys; and
now within its sacred walls his body was to rest,
until soul and body should be united again for
much higher worship and a more perfect blessedness in the sanctuary above. The spacious
galleries, so magnificent in their sweep, were filled
to their extremest capacity, and on almost every
face sat sorrow, wondering or weeping. The light
of mid-day was toned down to a melancholy dim-
ness by closely drawn blinds, and the solemn
obscurity was made still more solemn by lights
burning from the ceiling with a pale and sickly
lustre. The "Dead March in Saul" pealed forth
from the organ its touching strains of deep and
tender lamentation, wreathing its subtle harmonies
with the one solemn and regretful feeling that
pervaded the thousands present, as each pew in
succession, and every pew save one, received its
full contribution of a procession which moved on
and moved in as though it would never end. At
length, amid a stillness befitting the presence of
death, the mighty words of Scripture—announcing,
like a clarion note of victory, man's assured
deliverance from mortality and misery by a future
resurrection to eternal life and glory—were read
out with reverent emphasis by one whose friend-

ship with the departed had been the continuous joy of a long and honoured life. To these succeeded other words, human and feeble, but words of exhortation and comfort, spoken by a second, whose office at the time gave fitness to his discharge of a duty which must else have been committed to other hands; while, by a third, prayer was offered with so much solemnity and beseeching tenderness, that it carried the soul, though helpless yet hopeful, right into the presence of the Eternal Majesty. Finally, and immediately, without the interruption of a change of place, came those sublime utterances of human frailty and Divine mercy—of sorrow that weeps, while yet of faith that triumphs—with which we bid adieu to our sainted dead, and encourage even to full assurance the hope which looks onward to "the coming of our Lord Jesus Christ, and to our gathering together unto Him." Then arose in the heart the strange sad feeling that all was over. The hushed silence relieved itself in a low, sorrowful murmur. Hundreds, and even thousands, pressed to the grave side; and long was it ere the last look was taken of the place where lay all that death had now left behind of this once PRINCE IN ISRAEL.

I cannot, perhaps, more fittingly close these

"sketches" than by transcribing a few passages from the address delivered on the occasion of the funeral to the vast assembly gathered together to witness it. They are taken, with a few slight corrections, from the report given at the time in the public prints of the district.

"The Rev. J. Stacey, President of Conference, delivered the following address:—My Christian Friends,—I feel too profoundly the sad interest of this occasion to be able to command my thoughts in a suitable address; yet I would willingly say something appropriate to the solemnity, and which, by the blessing of God, may be the means of spiritual good to all present.

"Truly this is to us a day of lamentation; but I think I may add, and in this express your feelings as well as my own, that this lamentation is not unmingled with hope and joy. It is but a common event that has called us together, for 'man goeth to his long home, and the mourners go about the streets.' By the very law of his nature, 'man dieth and wasteth away.' And yet though common, there is surely something extraordinary in the event, or why our presence here in such large numbers, in such mournful display, in such solemn pomp? And something extraordinary there is: for a prince and a great man hath fallen—a prince in the church of

Christ, a great man according to any proper valuation of human character; a man ripe in years, but not riper in years than in wisdom, in virtue, in piety. We may therefore mourn as men, and we do mourn, and are not ashamed of our tears; but as Christian men we must rejoice, for it is written, 'Blessed are the dead which die in the Lord from henceforth. Yea, saith the Spirit, for they rest from their labours, and their works do follow them.'

"Can we doubt that this blessedness belongs to our beloved friend, who has just been taken from us? How true is it that he rests from his labours! In few cases are labours performed so long, so uninterruptedly, and in ways so various as were his. His activity was carried into every sphere of labour,—commercial, political, municipal, philanthropical, educational, religious; and into each with almost equal energy and success. How satisfactory is the thought that his last public labours, in so far as they were public—that his last labours on earth, in fact—were not commercial, were not political even, but strictly and properly religious; labours that concerned not immediately the interests of time, but interests that shall endure with still increasing freshness when time shall be no more. How fitting was the close of such a life! Who that knew, especially who that admired and loved him, would have desired for him a death other than the one he died? After labour, and in the very midst of labour, he sat down to rest; and his rest was made perpetual, because heavenly. The night came when work must cease, and the Lord gave him sleep: 'for so He giveth His beloved sleep.' The labour ceases, and all the outward signs of it too. The turmoil is at an end, and there is nothing to indicate that there has been turmoil; no sign of struggle, no indication of fatigue; no wearing sickness, or distressing pain; nothing but rest—the rest of the summer's eve, when the scythe and the sickle are laid aside, when the sheaves are bound up for the garner, and the shadow lies on the landscape where lately the sun has been. The outward is but the symbol of the higher and the lasting. He has, we may surely believe, rest in heaven—a rest which shall be eternal. Yet not the rest of inactivity, rather one of labour, though labour without fatigue and without sorrow. There is no pain to interrupt that rest, because there is no sin, nor disorder of any kind. It is rest in the full accord and perfect equilibrium of all the powers of the soul; especially in the satisfactions of Divine love and the glories of the Divine presence. 'In thy presence,' says the psalmist, 'is fulness of joy; at thy right hand are pleasures for evermore.'

"If, then, it is permitted to our beloved friend thus to rest, it is likewise permitted us to say, 'And his works do follow him.' Follow him they must in this life; for nothing that a man does ever dies. Everything perpetuates itself in some new form, enlarging its influence continually, like circles formed on a lake, long as time endures; and then, though breaking and dissolving on the shores of another world, yet commencing anew in other circles, of which eternity itself is the measure both of duration and increase. Thus shall the works of our friend follow him. And still, in another sense, shall they follow him. Purified from their dross, the fine gold shall follow him into the world above, and shall be there for enrichment and for treasure. With some abridgment of their bulk it may be, for he was human; with some deductions from their apparent value on the score of human frailty—perhaps with much—but, at the same time, with the very frailty forgiven, they shall follow him. That which is good cannot perish: it shall remain—not for merit, yet for reward; not as a plea to be urged, yet as a possession to be enjoyed. In so far as the works have been well done, the Saviour Judge shall say, 'Well done!' In so far as they have been done with reference to Him, with an eye directed to His glory, He will acknowledge them with approval, will breathe upon them the ever fragrant incense of His own merits, and graciously say, 'Thou hast done it unto me; enter into my joy!' Rejoice then, brethren and friends, even in the midst of your mourning.

> " ' Rejoice for a brother deceased,
>   Our loss is his infinite gain;
> A soul out of prison released,
>   And freed from his bodily chain.
> With songs let us follow his flight,
>   And mount with his spirit above:
> Escaped to the mansions of light,
>   And lodged in the Eden of love.
>
> " ' Our brother the haven hath gained,
>   Outflying the tempest and wind;
> His rest he hath surely obtained,
>   And left his companions behind
> Still toss'd on a sea of distress,
>   Hard toiling to make the bless'd shore,
> Where all is assurance and peace,
>   And sorrow and sin are no more.'

"As death brings us very near to eternity, and gives us an opportunity of solemn meditation, let us seize the present occasion for such thoughts as may well be suggested by it for our profit. If the life of him whose mortal remains we are about to commit to the earth, in sure and certain hope of a resurrection unto eternal life, teaches us anything, it teaches this especially, how much may be effected by varied and incessant labour. We live truly only as we work—'in deeds, not years; in thoughts, not breaths.' Wonderful was the activity of our departed friend: and they who would make most of life must in some measure live as he did; live and work in order to self-development, and for the profit of self-discipline; live and work in every fitting department of human enterprise, and for the public good. Of all work, religious work is the highest and most profitable. This was known and exemplified by him whose loss we this day mourn. Whatever good he did or obtained—his every success in life—was ever attributed by him to the blessing of God as the reward of early and continuous devotion to His service. And so of us, and of every one, religion is the first business and the chief blessedness. Man is great only by virtue of his moral and religious powers; and hence it is only by the sanctification and right employment of these that his true honour and happiness can be secured. 'Wisdom is the principal thing' is the testimony, everywhere repeated, of the Word of God. This testimony is given with almost equal clearness in the life of our friend; and what his life illustrates is applied and brought home with a still stronger emphasis by his death. The lesson thus taught is the one which *we* have to learn, and which, unless we learn it, or more fully realize its importance, from this solemnity, we shall miss the instruction which it is peculiarly fitted to give.

"But if this occasion reminds us of nothing else, it will surely remind us of this—that death is *our* lot too. Ah, brethren, there is no escaping from this. 'It is *appointed* unto man once to die.' It is the fixed, irreversible decree of Him who changeth not. Death is the most certain, while life is the most uncertain of all things. Its possible suddenness, as well as its inevitable certainty, is illustrated in the circumstances which have brought us to this place. Let each one then, young and old, receive the solemn admonition here addressed to him; especially those whose sun is fast hastening to its setting. Boast not thyself of to-morrow, boast not thyself of the next moment; for thou knowest not what the morrow, what the moment may bring forth. Instead of this, 'acquaint *now* thyself with Him, and be at peace; thereby good shall come unto thee.'

"And yet, once more, let me offer a word of encouragement to those who have obtained salvation through our Lord Jesus Christ, but who, perhaps, at times like this, look forward with sadness or with fear to their sure encounter with the last enemy. An enemy he is, but victorious he cannot be, where iniquity is forgiven and sin is pardoned. As only sin is the sting of death, when this is taken away—as in every case it is where faith unites the soul to Christ—death can have no sting at all. Let not the images under which death is sometimes presented rob you of your peace, or cloud for a moment your future prospect. Think not sadly of it, as of a valley into which no light enters, or a river of which the flood shall be only dark and violent. If to sense it is this, to faith it is far otherwise. And far otherwise shall be the reality. A valley gloomy and dreary it may be, but Christ's presence shall light it up. A river dark and stormy it sometimes is, but He who sitteth upon the waterfloods shall say, when your feet first touch its turbulent billows, 'Peace, be still.' To believers death is no real enemy, and shall at last have no positive terrors. It is rather the Lord's messenger of mercy come to entice and draw the soul away to His presence—come, with gentle pressure of their hand, to lead them right through the opened gate of the kingdom directly up to His throne.

"To all this is a time for serious and solemn reflection. The occasion will fail of its chief interest to us, if it does not make us thoughtful and prayerful; teaching us lessons that we can carry away with us, and improve in our daily duties and our daily pleasures. Death, I have said, brings eternity very near. It shuts out the world, gives a kind of retirement in which we can be alone with ourselves, and in this loneliness be alone also with God. For in truth, seldom are we so near to God and eternity as when death throws a shade upon all outward things—shows us their vanity and emptiness, hushes the noise of earthly business and earthly contentions, and turns our life for a season into silence and solitude. Let us enter still more deeply into this retirement which death has now made for us. Let us be alone with ourselves, or with only God for the witness and companion of our musings. And in this privacy of solemn thought let us make our own the words we have just read, each and all praying with an earnestness that ever wins the blessing that it seeks: 'So teach us to number our days, that we may apply our hearts unto wisdom.'"

www.ingramcontent.com/pod-product-compliance
Lightning Source LLC
Chambersburg PA
CBHW021204230426
43667CB00006B/555